And I Love You Still...

A Thoughtful Guide and Remembrance Journal for Healing the Loss of a Pet

Julianne C. Corbin, Ph.D.

And I Love You Still…A Thoughtful Guide and Remembrance Journal for Healing the Loss of a Pet

ISBN 987-1-7324044-1-0

Dedication

This book is dedicated to my Forever Girls, Cecilia and Bridgit, who graced my life in the most profound ways and bestowed eternal gifts to me that will forever light my path in the darkest of night. Your eternal golden spirits continue to sustain and inform every aspect of my life. My work is a lasting tribute to you. Rest in Peace, my sweet Golden Angels, until we meet again in fields of gold…I'll see you in my dreams…

Preface

For those fortunate to have experienced the deep bond and unconditional love of a companion animal, the death that follows can be one of the most difficult and misunderstood losses to go through. Even though companion animals are valued members of our family, this devastating loss frequently goes unrecognized, and is rarely taken with the seriousness it deserves. This loss is disregarded as insignificant and is trivialized by family, friends, and society, leaving grieving pet owners struggling with healthy coping methods and limited professional resources. Chances are if you are reading this book, you too have experienced the impact of this devastating loss. You understand, on a very personal level, that the grief experienced after losing a companion animal is minimized and dismissed with a pat on the back and suggestions to "just get another one."

Because of the disenfranchised nature of companion animal loss, there are few, if any, professionally written books or reflective journals addressing the difficulties unique to those grieving the loss of a beloved companion animal. When we lose a human loved one, we can expect to find countless resources and books written by Mental Health professionals, yet in the case of companion animal loss this is not so. While self-reported and anecdotal experiences are very helpful in validating and re-enfranchised one's loss, because of the complicated nature of companion animal loss, there is a need for professional and evidence-based information to help guide the grieving. *And I Love You Still: A Thoughtful Guide and Remembrance Journal for Healing the Loss of a Pet* fills this gap between the needs of grieving pet owners and the absence of professional support and resources available by presenting a professionally informed book and interactive reflective journal to help in understanding, validating, and processing through this tragic loss.

The inspiration for this book comes from both personal and professional experience. In my personal life, my canine companions have blessed me with the happiest and most treasured days of my life, and the sacred bond shared was truly magical. The devastating experience of loss and the isolating nature inherent in the grieving process made me acutely aware of the lack of awareness, sensitivity, and professional resources available to those grieving the loss of a companion animal and catalyzed my professional undertakings. As a Doctor of Clinical Psychology and Licensed Professional Counselor with 20 years of experience specializing in grief and traumatic loss, I witness, firsthand, the silent struggles and the detrimental emotional impact of grieving pet owners who are marginalized from supports typically available after a human loss. To help meet the needs of grieving pet owners, in 2005, I founded Pet Loss Support Services of NJ which provides; clinical, supportive, and educational services on all aspects of the Human-Animal Bond and Companion Animal Loss. In 2006, I completed my Ph.D. dissertation research entitled: *"A Phenomenological Study of Canine loss and Grief Response: Clinical and Depth Psychological Implications,"* which serves as a framework for this book and is the go-to resource and guide for Mental Health Professionals working with grieving pet owners. In 2018, I published *"Beyond the Horizon: A Remembrance Journal for Healing the Loss of a Pet,"* which is a reflective and therapeutic journal assisting grieving pet owners in processing and healing their loss.

May this informative book and reflective journal provide much-needed guidance and comfort during your time of loss. Peace to all.

Introduction

Written by Licensed Psychotherapist, Researcher, and renowned expert on the Human-Animal Bond and Companion Animal Loss, Dr. Corbin brings the consulting room to your fingertips in this groundbreaking, one of a kind book and reflective journal. Drawing on 20 years of clinical, research, and personal experience, Dr. Corbin explores the bond shared between humans and their companion animals and calls attention to the difficulties unique to this overlooked and disenfranchised loss. *And I Love You Still: A Thoughtful Guide and Remembrance Journal for Healing the Loss of a Pet* is both a book and therapeutic journal filled with valuable information on the once-in-a-lifetime bond we share with our companion animals and the traumatizing grief that follows.

Each chapter begins with an in-depth discussion and thoughtful reflections offering tips and recommendations for coping, shares real-life stories of love, loss, and healing, and then transitions to a set of therapeutic questions intended to elicit personal memories, reflections, insights, and healing. Because the death of a beloved companion animal can be a very difficult and personal experience, you may find there are occasions when it can be too difficult to talk about your feelings with others. During these times, it can be therapeutic to engage in reflective writing or journal therapy to help attain a deeper understanding of your emotional process and gain emotional clarity. Use the journal part of this book to create a healing and sacred space where you can openly express your thoughts, feelings, and most profound emotions of loving and losing your beloved animal companion without judgment or shame. This journal will allow you to reflect on your relationship and grieving process and how your experience changes over time and serves as a "linkage" that connects you to your beloved companion animal.

Chapters One and Two begins by exploring the nature of the Human-Animal Bond. Through clinical experience, research, and real-life anecdotal stories, it illustrates the many ways this relationship enriches and informs our lives. Dr. Corbin thoughtfully guides you to reflect and reminisce on the special bond shared with your beloved companion animal throughout the years and provides a framework to help you express and capture your most intimate thoughts and feelings about your bond and relationship.

Chapters Three and Four moves on to the topic of companion animal loss and discusses, through clinical experience, research, and real-life anecdotal stories, the unique difficulties inherent in this complicated and disenfranchised loss. Using therapeutic questions and prompts, Dr. Corbin guides you through the stages commonly experienced following the death of a companion animal, allowing you to reflect on and explore your subjective experiences, thoughts, and feelings.

Throughout this book, Dr. Corbin challenges many of the myths associated with a companion animal's death and discusses the impact of this disenfranchised loss on our emotional and psychological well-being. Providing a much-needed respite of healing and comfort during your difficult time of loss, this book and remembrance journal guides you in understanding, reflecting, and processing important topics such as:

- **The Healing Power of the Human-Animal Bond:** Based on clinical, research, and personal experience Dr. Corbin provides real-life examples and discusses the distinctive and unique qualities that define the relationship and bond shared with our companion animals, shedding light on the difficulties inherent in the loss.

- **Our Life and Journey Together: From Day One Until the End:** With the use of journal prompts and questions, Dr. Corbin guides you to recall treasured memories about your beloved and relationship throughout your time together, from your first days till the end.

- **Pet Loss and Disenfranchised Grief:** Helping answer why the death of a companion animal can be so challenging and provides tips, real-life examples, and journal questions and prompts to help you work through your individual experience.

- **Pet Loss and Complicated Grief:** For some bereaved pet owners, grief can be overwhelming and complicated, leading to a wide range of symptoms. Learn what is considered "normal" and what is not. Provides suggestions for coping, real-life examples, and journal prompts and questions for processing difficult emotions.

- **Stages of Grief Following the Death of a Pet:** Discusses and guides you through stages commonly experienced after the death of a companion animal such as: Shock and Disbelief, Painful Emotions, Living in the Past, and Acceptance & Reconciliation. With the help of real-life examples, therapeutic prompts, and questions, Dr. Corbin supports you through these common stages and associated feelings, thoughts, and reactions, helping you to gain insight and healing.

- **Memorializing, Commemorating, and Other Topics Specific to Healing the Loss of a Companion Animal.**

And I Love You Still: A Thoughtful Guide and Remembrance Journal for Healing the Loss of a Pet is written in tribute to all the companion animals who have graced our lives in ways only we could know. May this book and reflective journal help you come to a place of comfort and healing in your journey towards healing.

Table of Contents

CHAPTER ONE:

The Human-Animal Bond

Introduction: The Human-Animal Bond and Beyond

And even after all this time, the sun never says to the earth, "you owe me." Look what happens to a love like that. It lights up the whole sky – Hafiz

Approximately 85 million families have companion animals in the United States (APPA), yet many people still do not understand the emotional, psychological, and spiritual significance of the human-animal bond and continue to trivialize the impact of companion animal loss. How many times have you been told in response to your loss that; "it's just a dog or cat," "just get another one," "why are you not over it yet," or "you know pets don't live as long as humans do "? These insensitive and disenfranchising comments in response to companion animal loss illustrate the ignorance that prevails in our society, even today, regarding the significance of the human-animal bond. It is not so much whether our loss is human or animal but more about the nature and meaning of our relationship to and with the deceased that informs our grief. If we are to understand why the loss of a companion animal can be one of the most challenging events of our life, we need to consider the extraordinary bond and multidimensional relationship we share with our companion animals.

Those who have been graced by the presence of a companion animal in their lives can appreciate that there are as many reasons to love them as there are stars in the sky! Each beloved companion animal brings something unique and magical to that era of our lives. They touch us and perhaps change us in a way nothing or no one else ever could. Being so much more than "pets," they are treasured family members, we acknowledge their contribution to individual and family morale, we derive closeness to, accept responsibility for, and share activities with, we become emotionally devoted to them and, naturally, we grieve when they die. Our companion animals are faithful, reliable, devoted, comforting, loyal, trustworthy, gentle, kind, and the ultimate knower of love. Our relationship with them is deep and wide; to us, they are not "like" our children; they ARE our children. We see and interact with them more than some family members or friends, we are their world, and they are ours. Our companion animals were there for us when we needed someone, we were with them from their beginning to their end, and perhaps for the first time in our lives, we experienced unconditional love and positive regard. The depth and nature of our relationship with our companion animals may be like no other relationship in life and when they die, it can leave a hole in our life the size of the Grand Canyon.

From human loss, we know that the stronger the bond and deeper the relationship, the harder the loss, and the death of a companion animal is no exception to this rule. In my research on the Human-Canine Bond and Pet Loss (2006), relational themes were identified through a detailed data analysis of complex interviews, which underscored the relationship between humans and canine companions. These themes are confirmed in my clinical psychotherapy practice and help shine a light on why the grieving process is such a traumatizing event. These themes will be discussed in the following pages and include:

- The spiritual connection we share with our companion animals

- How our companion animals act as our secure base and transitional guides through difficult life events.

- How we experience the bond and relationship with our companion animals as a source of unconditional love and positive regard.

- The many mental and physical health benefits we derive from the human-animal bond.

The relationship with our companion animals is unique to human bonds and is multi-dimensional; they are much more than "pets" to us and function in many different capacities in our lives. In so many ways, they support, heal and protect us; they see parts of us that perhaps no one else will ever witness. When our companion animals die, we lose many different relationships wrapped into one beautiful and sacred package.

Spiritual Connection and the Human - Animal Bond

One of the aspects that makes the bond with our companion animals unique and the loss particularly difficult is the deep spiritual connection many people experience. By their very nature dogs and other companion animals seem to have an innate ability to connect to others on a heart to heart and soul to soul level, as if they can see into the very core of our being! The relationship with our companion animals can be a reflection or reminder of our own sense of the spiritual and can mirror what is missing in ourselves and our lives. Our deep-seated desire for love, closeness, and affiliation with nature is what draws so many of us to our companion animals and what makes the bond so extraordinary. By their very nature, dogs and cats remind us of a fundamental wisdom which oftentimes eludes us; they are masters in the kingdom of now, being fully present to the simple pleasures in life and each moment, they know only the present and offer themselves to it without reservation. Those "simple" pleasures in life somehow are not all that simple, yet our companion animals are tuned in so instinctively to those things. Companion animals can help us connect more deeply with nature and the natural world through what Biologist Edward O. Wilson calls "Biophilia." Biophilia suggests that we, as humans, possess an innate drive to seek connections with nature and affiliate with other forms of life. Perhaps our bond with companion animals can be understood as a draw towards re-connecting to the natural world from which modern civilization separates us. Through engagement with our companion animals, we are given an opportunity to connect with nature and the natural world. Freud, Jung, and other psychologists have implied that man's existential crisis comes from our detachment from our "ancestral environment," or nature from which we evolved. It is only within the last few decades that we have begun to understand the human-animal bond and its connection to something bigger than ourselves, something beyond the human condition.

We have shaped nature and nature has shaped us, making us an emergent property of this relationship. It is not surprising that our need for connecting with the natural world includes animals and our relationship with them. However, as our world becomes more urbanized, overpopulated, and technology-driven, person-to-person interaction and contact with nature is less significant in everyday life. Social media has replaced "real-time" friendships, handshakes, and hugs, and the internet age will continue to facilitate a fundamental shift in interpersonal relations. People separating from one another leaves something missing; something core to our existence, and our beloved companion animals fill this gap. Although domesticated, companion animals are still relatively "wild" with senses and abilities that make them suited for survival in nature, and our close relationship with them keeps nature very present in our lives, reminding us of the importance of slowing down, disconnecting, and simply "being" in the here and now. Our companion animals have a way of bringing us back those things most important yet most easily forgotten like; a first snowfall, flowers blooming on a Spring day, the sunrise and the sunset, the sound of falling leaves, the smell of freshly cut grass, the sound of rain falling, etc. In their short lives, through aging and illness, and into their death, our companion animals are a constant reminder and reflection of what faith, hope, and love are really about. If our eyes are open, they can teach us something about living in the moment and allow us to comprehend the idea of refuge and personal sanctuary and the importance of slowing down and being mindful. Within these moments reflected to us by our companion animals, we can see with a new perspective the natural beauty and wisdom of the world around us and appreciate our connection to it.

Real Life Vignettes of Spiritual Connection and the Human-Animal Bond

Following are real-life narratives taken from clinical, research, and book interviews that highlight the spiritual bond we share with our companion animals. These are just a few examples of how grieving pet owners describe their experience of deep and profound connection, and perhaps you might find validation, hope, and connection through these brief vignettes.

Julianne C. and Canine Companion Cecilia:

If there is one lesson I have learned from Cecilia, it is life in the glorious moment of "now" is what makes every day a miracle. I have learned many things in the ten years I have been graced with her presence, but it was during those final and most unpredictable days that I learned what it meant to be truly alive. She taught me how to exist within the experience of uncertainty. Through her, I learned that in order to be truly alive, one must feel the grasp of finality. Our world had shifted from the news of her cancer; our world became smaller and more compact. We could no longer take our daily hikes and runs through nature, so instead, we sat in the back yard looking over the creek to the trails behind our home. I remember sitting, angry, crying, hoping, praying, and trying to understand why she became ill. Then I would look to Cecilia sitting by my side, and she was none of those things; she did not know of those things. She just knew that the sun was out, the wind was blowing, the birds were chirping and it was a great day. She may or may not have known of her upcoming journey, but one thing was for sure; she truly lived in the here and now, taking in everything that made life worth living in that very moment. Cecilia always had a way to bring me back those things most important yet most easily forgotten.

Joyce T. and Canine Companion Toby:

I have always felt a strong spiritual connection to animals, especially dogs. I believe that our canine companions can mirror what is missing in ourselves and our lives and remind us to be more present. I have always found that to be what has drawn me to dogs; they remind me that there is so much more beyond the material things that seem to define who and what we are. In our daily hikes together, he would help me to connect to nature's beauty. Forcing me to shut the phone off and connect in and outward at the same time. Toby was my connection to nature and all its divine glory. He reminded me to be present, and he always me back to base, back to my core when I would get too far away. I think that is what I miss most about Toby. I use to joke around and call him my Z Man, Z for Zen. I miss my Z Man.

Clair W. and Canine Companion Penny:

Penny brought a sense of the sacred to me. I am a spiritual person by nature, so I have that antenna up all the time, but I never expected to get that from a dog. She enriched my spiritual life by reminding me to take it slow, stop, and look around. Penny naturally did those things that I try so very hard to accomplish, creating a sense of serenity. Penny was my meditation partner, and I mean literally. I would put the music on, bring the mat out, and she would sit in meditation with me. I almost felt an obligation not to miss my daily meditation because if I did, she would let me know it was time! She really was special, and our spiritual connection was more than words could ever describe.

Michael L. and Canine Companion Freddie:

Freddie seemed to be connected to a part of life that I became slowly estranged from without even realizing it. As he got older, he became so tuned in to his environment and would get great pleasure from just sitting outside looking over his "domain." Freddie seemed content just sitting and "being." That is something I desperately needed back in my life, and by example, he brought me back to that spiritual space. In the last couple of years of his life, he became so noble as if he knew things I did not, and I really believe he was my teacher of sorts. What stands out for me and our bond is how Freddie taught me and reminded me of the importance of being in the moment, slowing down, and taking it all in. That was his gift to me and I will always love him for that.

Sue P. and Canine Companion Lacey:

Lacey was forgiving, nonjudgmental, always happy to see us and, most of all, she loved unconditionally and with all her heart and soul. Love was the basis for her happiness and her existence. Lacey taught me by example what faith, hope, and love really look like. She taught me to give up control and how to pray, not with desperation but rather with acceptance. Towards her final days, she taught me how to still be happy and excited over the simple things like an ice cream cone even though it may be your last, how her soul would still smile each and every time she saw those she loved, even though she was in pain and dying. It was never about her or what she was going through; it was about life and love and expressing that love at every single opportunity she was given. She strengthened my spiritual being because she lived each day with a unique quality of life, each hour with the outlook that there was no end in sight, therefore no reason to be sad. She helped me understand hope in a new light with each stage of her illness. She just continued to live, and I saw the hope in her eyes for a new day and a better tomorrow. Now that she is at peace, I am lost without her yet much richer because of her. What more of an everlasting gift of the spirit could she give me?

Jill B. and Canine Companion Erin:

Erin experienced every day as if it was her first and her last as if everything she experienced was for the first time. She seemed to love instinctively without thought or expectation, and she just "was." Throughout her life, she showed me the importance of the simple things in life; she forced me to slow down and just breathe. You know that great big sigh at the end of the day? Well, she was my great big sigh. When she became ill, she embraced her fateful reality without judgment or fear; she simply accepted things as they were and learned how to make the best of her final days. That is the legacy she leaves me: accepting and embracing life's circumstances that we cannot change. I think that the spiritual connection we had is what I miss the most because I never had that with anyone else in my life.

Comfort Companions: Our Secure Base and Transitional Guides

A therapeutic quality inherent in the human-animal bond is how companion animals become our secure base and act as guides during life's most challenging and difficult times. Like a warm blanket on a cold night, they provide warmth and safety from a world that can be cold and harsh. Companion animals are our comfort soothers in the face of life transitions, uncertainties, and traumatic events such as; the death of a spouse, family member, or friend, divorce, marriage, personal illness or injury, loss of a job, retirement, moving, children leaving home, etc. They seem to always be there for us in times of need, and unlike human relationships, their love does not wax and wane. They are predictable in their response to us, provide a cocoon of protection when we need it the most, and become our "anchor" amid crisis. By their very nature and without question, companion animals become our "secure base" by bestowing us with comfort, security, consistency, stability, reliability, self-soothing/self-calming functions, and emotional support during moments when we need it the most.

Companion animals, however, are much more than a "substitute" for human interaction or a mirror of human relationships. For example, companion animals can function as a "transitional object" by providing the framework for consistency and predictability in a world that, for some, may be experienced as unstable and chaotic. Unlike other relationships in our lives, some companion animals have the inherent ability to sense our emotional and psychological needs and respond in a way that makes us feel safe and secure. This aspect of the human-animal bond is especially significant for those who have experienced personal trauma, abuse, or certain psychological conditions because it creates a holding environment of trust and protection in the same way a maternal figure might and serves as a secure base whereby transitions and changes are safe. For others, the relationship with their companion animal may symbolize an absent person to whom they were once attached and who provided emotional and psychological support during times of change and crisis. In my psychotherapy practice working with emotionally, psychologically, and physically abused clients, dogs serve as a vital transitional guide allowing them to form healthy attachments with other living beings in place of those relationships which have been traumatic in early life. The role of companion animals as transitional objects and guides provides a sense of safety and comfort in the otherwise tenuous and unpredictable lives of those in abusive relationships. The dog "object," the symbolic nature of the relationship, becomes incorporated and internalized into the self-structure and becomes a building block to healthier self-esteem and sense of self.

Our deep attachment to companion animals' also echoes a collective need to lessen the relentless shock of overwhelming changes and uncertainties in today's fast-paced and technology-driven world. There is a loss of security in today's society, loss of interpersonal and social bonds, and loss of connection to nature that leaves us in need of transitional guides that help cushion the devastation of these losses in our lives. We may find that "transitional" guide in our companion animals as they so instinctively become surrogate nurturers in place of community and social structures, which at one time filled these roles. Our companion animals have the natural ability to roll with the changes and be that one predictable thing we can always count on in a world of swift change. They shepherd us through some of our darkest and most unpredictable moments and ask for so little in return. When we lose a companion animal, we lose much more than a "pet"; we are losing a relationship that is woven in a tapestry of security, stability, bountiful love, and selfless giving.

.

Real Life Vignettes of Creature Comforts: Companion Animals as our Secure Base and Transitional Guide

Following are real-life narratives taken from clinical, research, and book interviews that highlight how our companion animals can serve as our secure base and transitional guides during difficult and transitory times in our lives. These are just a few examples of how grieving pet owners describe their experience of deep and profound connection, and perhaps you might find validation, hope, and connection through these brief vignettes.

Claire W. and Canine Companion Penny:

When I think about Penny, what I miss most about her is how she would somehow make me feel so calm. Her presence was so comforting to me. Being with her was like taking a big deep sigh, especially when things got really tough in my family; she would instinctively know what my needs were and could provide comfort without words. I could always count on her, and she was the one constant in my life, always there when others failed me. I think it was not until she died that I realized how much she gave me. In her own doggie way, she protected me from the world. After a long day, I would come home, and she could read my mood and respond soothingly. With her, the world felt safe somehow. No matter how many crazy things happened in my day or my life, I knew that I could come home to Penny and know exactly what to expect, no surprises there. She just kept me safe.

Carol U. and Feline Companion Chelsea:

Chelsea has been with me through every trial and tribulation of my life, just everything. She was the one thing that was always constant. The absolute thing I could rely on was Chelsea; my family is very cold and very emotionally distant. So, for me, having Chelsea was the first time in my life that I was able to love anything and receive love in return. In my house growing up, there was no consistency whatsoever. I had gone through so much with Chelsea by my side; divorce, illness, moving, etc., and she was a constant support for me during those times. Chelsea provided consistency and stability for me in a world that felt very turbulent and erratic. Her presence sustained me through all the tumultuous times in my life and gave me a sense of security that I had never had before. There are no words to describe how much I miss her.

Rachael Z. and Canine Companion Charlie:

Charlie was my security blanket in my unstable and erratic world and was the first thing in my life to bridge that gap for me. I have gone through many bad relationships and many changes in my life. I never had any stability, even growing up. Charlie was always there to bring me a sense of stability; he was that one stable force in my life. I had many transitions in a 10-year period, and he would just go with the changes and keep me balanced and grounded. He was my giant teddy bear that would keep me safe and kept me secure in the midst of so many changes. No person had ever done that for me before. I feel so lost without him; like a small child lost in a world that is too big.

Christine C. and Canine Companion Sunny:

I have always been in the midst of change; for some reason my life has never been very constant. Moving every year, changing jobs, losing loved ones, etc.

Just as I would begin to feel the ground under my feet, something would pull the carpet out from under me. That is where Sunny came into play. No matter how crazy things were around me, she would always be the same; she never changed. Her love and affection were the one thing I could count on in my life to always be there; to always get me through the day. As I would go from one job to the next, from one relationship to the next, from one move to the next, Sunny was the only thing that remained untouched by the hands of time. She was my constant source of stability, and now that she is gone, I do not know if I will ever feel that safe feeling again.

Heather R. and Canine Companion Clarence:

I have been plagued with many illnesses since I was a child, and I was in and out of foster care. Never in one place for too long, so my background does not have a lot of security. Clarence was the first thing that I could count on to always be there for me. He seemed to take on the role of the consistent caretaker. He knew when I was sick and what to do. I knew that no matter what happened during the course of my day, when I would come home, he would be there for me and in his own doggy way, would take care of me. He was like the parent I never had, like the sibling I never had. It was the security of knowing that he would always be there, no matter how bad things became in my life, no matter how many tests and different medications I had to be on. He was that one steady and predictable thing in my life I could always count on. I never had that before I found Clarence, or maybe I should say before Clarence found me. He was my rock and made me feel secure. I am learning how to do this for myself now that he is gone, but it is not the same; it will never be the same.

Callie T. and Canine Companion Psalms:

I am a twin, and we have been roommates since conception. We were together in preschool, elementary, middle, high school, college and after college. So, imagine my devastation when my sister announced that she wanted to move out of the house we shared together. It was as if someone pulled the carpet from under my feet! Psalms helped me with this difficult change and transition. She was my little sidekick, buddy, my little ride or die. Psalms took away the loneliness and devastation. She also helped me when my father was diagnosed with cancer, and my cousin committed suicide. She was the one thing I could always count on to be there to help me stay grounded and centered. She was also there to help me after a terrible accident. Psalms, Proverbs, and I were driving from Pa to NC for Christmas holiday. While driving down interstate 95, a car veered into my lane. Psalms and Proverbs were reading my energy, so I remained calm and answered questions from the cops and fire department. They wanted to take me to the hospital, but I refused to leave my dogs in VA on the side of the road. It took several hours to receive my rental car and continue my drive to NC. The drive to NC was one of the hardest things I've had to endure because I was afraid to drive after my collision. I was crying and shaking during the drive, and Psalms and Proverbs proceeded to cry and whine during the drive. Psalms was staring at me as if to say, "you have this mommy, you can do this because you are my hero" (that sounds cheesy, but she always looked at me like that). Her faith in me gave me the strength to continue on. Through every post-accident obstacle and difficult time, I would always hug her or she would do something calming and soothing to decrease my stress and bring me peace and comfort.

Marcie S. and Canine Companion Shayna:

Shayna was with me through so many difficult and as well as happy major life events. I lost her when she was just two weeks shy of her 15th birthday. When I think about it, that was almost a third of my life. She was with me through some very significant and impactful losses in my life. First, the loss of my Grandmother in 2000, and then eight years later, the sudden loss of my mother in 2008. Both of these losses were extremely difficult, and Shayna was always there to comfort me and always by my side; sort of the "stable" force in my life. No matter how sad I was at any given time, Shayna always made me smile and feel comforted; she was "home" to me. I also met and married my wonderful husband during her life. He lived in a different state, so that involved quitting my job, selling my home, and moving out of state. Again, even though it was a happy event, it was a huge transition, but there was Shayna, right by my side every step of the way. It felt like having my best friend with me at all times. How great is that? I remember driving up to NJ from VA to settle on our new home. It was an exciting and scary time for me as these were huge changes for me to move away from my home, family, friends, job, etc. Shayna was my rock once again, always with me, always my stable force. Sometimes it felt like there wasn't much that I could count on, but her love and companionship was certainly the one thing I could. I felt like she was "witness" to such major events in my life, even more than my Mom who was no longer with me. I married late in life, and one of my regrets was that my Mother never saw me get married, but Shayna did and she loved her new "Daddy."

A Sacred Bond and Relationship: The Source of Unconditional Love and Positive Regard

The relationship with our companion animals encompasses some of the strongest and deepest bonds known to human life. To us, our beloved companion animals are much more than pets; they are; family members, surrogate children, best friends, daily companion, mother, twin, partner, and so much more. They are the quintessential example of unconditional love, unconditional positive regard, trust, and safety. By their very nature, companion animals provide a wellspring of acceptance and support and offer us a profound and deep connection to another living being, which is not always found in human relationships. Companion animals bear witness to ourselves and our lives in ways others may not. They see the part of us that the rest of the world may not; they see us at our worst, they see us at our best, and everything in between. When our companion animals depart this life, one of the things we say good-bye to is the presence of a "*living witness*" to our most intimate and authentic selves. Not only do our companion animals give us their uninhibited and most natural emotional expression and reactions, but they also allow *us* the space and security to express parts of ourselves in ways we might otherwise not. The death of our companion animal can mean the loss of this "living witness" that accepted, without judgment, our weaknesses, fragilities, vulnerabilities, and failures as well as our uniqueness, strengths, victories, and successes. If we are fortunate, they accompany and shepherd us through the years of our lives and define an era that will forever remain sacred to us. This sacred relationship and rich bond we share with our companion animals helps us understand why it is so traumatizing when they are gone from our lives. The level of emotional intimacy shared with them is not always felt with human family members.

It is this deep level of connection and attachment which is at the very core of the pain we experience when they die. When our companion animals depart, we say good-bye to many different relationships contained in one small yet profound package of unconditional love and positive regard. It is never "just" a dog or "just" cat, etc. It is so much more, and recognizing this can help us not question or minimize our grief.

While this book speaks to the bonds we share with companion animals and the grief experienced after a loss, it is helpful to consider the relationship between service dogs and humans to understand further the power of the human-animal bond and the impact of loss. There are more than 22,000 individuals in the United States who are partnered with a service dog. This partnership has been shown to have significant benefits for the owner such as: increased ability to perform daily living activities, positive impact on one's psychological and emotional health, and increased participation in social, work, school, and activities outside the home. Service dogs become the eyes, ears, hands, and legs for those with disabilities, becoming an "extension" of the person they are assisting. This lends itself to a powerful relationship and resilient bond built on trust, safety, and security. Additionally, PTSD trained service dogs for military veterans can recognize and interrupt early signs of anxiety, panic, panic attacks, and nightmares. This helps veterans break the cycle of retraumatization, redirect their focus, and regain emotional control in certain situations. Not only are PTSD service dogs trained to help manage symptoms and provide soothing and comfort during an episode, but they are also able to prevent an episode from occurring. A recent study by Purdue University College of Veterinary Medicine found that military veterans with PTSD formed an unusually strong bond with their service dogs, which supports the idea that service dogs are extraordinary at helping military veterans heal from and overcome PTSD. The intense bond shared between veterans and canines is something all dog lovers can understand and relate to, but this research suggests that the bond may far exceed that of a companion animal relationship. This critical study brings us one step closer to scientifically understanding and demonstrating that service dogs are an effective therapeutic intervention for veterans and others diagnosed with PTSD and validates the sacred bond and relationship we all have experienced.

For many grieving pet parents, a companion animal/service dog's death can be more difficult than that of a close family member or friend and frequently struggle with feelings of intense guilt and shame over the severity of their grief. However, in the context of the multifaceted, unique, and sacred bond shared with our companion animals, it should be no surprise that the grief following a death is profound and life-changing. You should not feel guilty or ashamed about your intense grief, nor should you question if what you feel is normal. As you work through your grieving process, always remember that it is not whether your loss was human or animal; it is the *nature of your bond and the depth of your attachment* that underscores your experience.

Real Life Vignettes of Our Sacred Bond and Relationship: The Source of Unconditional Love and Positive Regard

Following are real-life narratives taken from clinical, research, and book interviews that highlight our sacred bond and relationship and how our companion animals are a source of unconditional love and positive regard. These are just a few examples of how grieving pet parents describe their experience of deep and profound connection, and perhaps you might find validation, hope, and connection through these brief vignettes.

Mark D. and Feline Companion Pearl:

Pearl was always by my side, and her nickname was "little velcro." You would have thought that some invisible cord attached us; both physically, emotionally, and spiritually. I think I was more attached to her than to any human in my life. I've always had a hard time trusting people, so I would never form strong bonds of attachment. With Pearl, it was so easy; she was so trustworthy that I began bonding with her, and next thing you know, for the first time in my life, I felt a real connection to someone. Physically we were always together. She would always be by me at the piano as I played and wrote my music. Emotionally, we were attached in such a way that she brought great joy into my life and filled many vacant spots inside me. Spiritually, we were connected; like the time when I knew she was in trouble and I ran home to help her, or when I knew she was ill and I felt it myself on a visceral level, or when she was dying, I felt this pang in the car and drove home to find her waiting for me to take her last breath. We were just so attached on many levels, and I do not think I will ever experience that kind of relationship ever again.

Michelle O. and Canine Companion Autumn:

Autumn was a Therapy Dog, and she came everywhere with me; she was a part of every aspect of my life. Not just get up in the morning, feed the dog, go to work, come home, feed, and walk the dog. No, she was with me almost 24/7, and that worked for us. I think because of this, we developed an amazingly close attachment to each other. She would react if I were gone too long, and I would never leave her alone for more than a few hours at a time, even when she was healthy. My husband would say it was like I was married to Autumn and more connected to her than him, and maybe he was right. We were very attached, and that bond became even stronger as she got older and then began dying. The attachment grew to the point to where I did not know where she ended and I began. I know this may sound odd, but it was like we merged together as one. Towards the end of her life, I could read her so well, and she myself and that's what hurts so bad. How can I ever sever that bond, that attachment I have with Autumn? She filled up so many parts of my life that I feel like half a person without her. My life seemed to have been dictated by the degree of attachment we had for each other. It was just something really special and maybe a bit over the top, but like I said, it worked for me.

June B. and Feline Companion Ziggy:

In addition to the source of unconditional love, I think what is most significant thing about our relationship is that he somehow snuck his way into my heart and soul without me ever knowing it. I never really trusted people, but Ziggy...Ziggy taught me how to trust, and because of that, for the first time in my life, I allowed myself to actually become close to someone or something. For the first time in my life, I knew what it felt like to feel a connection to something, a bond to something. I always prided myself in not being attached to anything, but that was just a disguise. I was lonely and scared to connect with someone. With Ziggy, that safe connection grew into the most amazing and trusting attachment that I have ever felt in my life. He taught me how to trust, feel safe, and allow myself to be open up and take in love. I am hoping in time, I will be able to take that lesson and apply it to other areas of my life. That it is okay to be open and to love, and that connection is not a sign of weakness. Even in his death, I still feel such a strong connection and attachment to him, and I know I always will.

Sam V. and Canine Companion Rusty:

Rusty was the biggest part of our family in that we involved her in all of our activities, and she was the center of attention. She was not just a "dog"; she was an integral part of our family. My wife and I do not have children; we are childless by choice. When we got Rusty, now looking back, having her brought out our maternal instincts, and it was so fulfilling that we did not desire anything different or more. But she was more than a surrogate child; and she was my best friend and my companion. My wife travels a lot for her job, so when she would be gone, it would be Rusty and me, like a child, best friend, and companion all in one. That's 3 in 1. I never had human children, but to me, this was fatherhood; I don't care what anyone says. No matter how I looked or felt, she would be there all the same. I guess that is what unconditional love is all about. She exuded unconditional love, and it came naturally from her. Without thought or preconceived notions; she was unconditional love in its truest form. That also made the relationship so special and deeply missed. I think it's such a hard thing with us pet owners because they've become our child. I think especially with people who don't have children like myself, they really become like our children, and you have to watch them grow old in front of you, slowly die in front of you.

Carol M. and Feline Companion Summer:

Summer filled in so many pieces of my life. As a single, childless, 30 something year old woman, I do not have that husband, 2.5 children, and picket fence. Summer became my family because my human family lives very far away. So, it became Summer and I; we were family. She was the source of love that had no end , like it just went around in circles. In addition to her being like my child, she was also a source of unconditional love, which you do not get from human children; she became the family that I dearly miss that is so far away. We just understood each other so well and she was always there for me. Human children are not these things, so the way I see it losing Summer, losing any animal dear to our hearts is more difficult be cause we lose so mu ch more. She was more than my pet; she was my first child. Losing her was like losing a part of me, and although it's one year later, it is still so hard for me. I'll never know a love like the love she unconditionally gave to me. The level of loyalty she had for me was so great that I couldn't conceive ever getting that from another; whether human or otherwise. I wish that she was still in my life, and I struggle many days without her. I will never forget her and the special once-in-a-lifetime relationship we shared.

Mental and Physical Health Benefits of the Human-Animal Bond

Anyone reading this book is familiar with the immediate joys that come with sharing their lives with a companion animal; however, many may not be aware of the physical and mental health benefits that can accompany the pleasure of snuggling up with our four-legged furry companion. All of the ways in which companion animals enrich our lives emotionally, physically, and spiritually positively impact our mental and physical health. I have seen firsthand in my psychotherapy practice the therapeutic benefits of what research shows; that the companionship a pet offers can help us live healthier lives and cope with depression, anxiety, panic, stress, mood disorders, eating disorders, and PTSD. Studies on the mental and physical benefits of companion animal ownership show that:

- People with pets have lower blood pressure in stressful situations as compared to those without pets.

- People with pets are less likely to suffer from depression than those without pets. Those with a history of depression scored lower on the Beck Depression Inventory after just six months of pet ownership.

- People with pets report lower levels of anxiety, loneliness, and isolation than those without pets.

- Stroking, hugging, or touching a loving pet can rapidly calm and soothe you when you're depressed, stressed, or anxious, reduce muscle tension, lower pulse rate, and provide sensory stress relief.

- Playing with a dog or cat can elevate serotonin levels, dopamine, and oxytocin levels, which reduces stress and anxiety.

- People with pets have lower triglyceride and cholesterol levels than those without pets.

- Heart attack patients with pets survive longer than those without a pet.

- People with pets are more likely to engage in a daily exercise routine of walking, hiking, or jogging.

- Pet owners over the age of 65 make 30 percent fewer visits to their doctors than those without pets.

- Pets can help decrease loneliness and help us be more social and meet new people.

Source: Harvard Health Publications

Companion animals can also play an integral role in the health of the elderly by helping to:

- **Find meaning and purpose in life.** As we age, it is normal to experience the loss of things that previously gave our life purpose and meaning. Retiring from your career, loss of mobility, your children moving far away, and empty nest syndrome can all create an existential crisis for many aging folks. Caring for a pet can bring a sense of purpose and meaning to your life and boost your morale, optimism, and self-worth.

- **Stay connected**. Maintaining social connections becomes more difficult as we grow older, and making new friends can become difficult. Things such as retirement, illness, death, and relocation can leave the aging feeling alone and isolated. Companion animals, especially dogs, are a great way for older adults to spark up conversations, meet new people, and get involved in social activities.

- **Boost your health and vitality.** You can slow down many of the physical challenges associated with aging by tending to your emotional well-being. Dogs and cats encourage playfulness, laughter, and exercise, which has been shown to help boost immunity, increase energy, and support overall health.

- **Companion animals help patients with Alzheimer's Disease.** Alzheimer's patients may exhibit a variety of behavioral problems, some of these problems are primary to the disease, and some may be related to an inability to manage stress effectively. Researchers at the University of California at Davis (2010) found that Alzheimer's patients experience less stress and have fewer anxious or angry outbursts if there is a dog or cat in their home. Because companion animals provide a source of unconditional positive regard, unconditional love, and nonverbal communication, the playful interaction and gentle touch from a gentle companion animal can help soothe an Alzheimer's patient and decrease aggressive or problematic behaviors.

Source: Harvard Health Publications

Throughout history, pets have evolved to become highly attuned to their human companions' emotions and behaviors, which is one reason therapy dogs are prevalent in hospitals, nursing homes, and hospice and are especially helpful for those with disabilities and special needs. Dogs (especially service dogs and therapy dogs) can understand many of the words we use. Still, they're even better at interpreting and responding positively to our tone of voice, body language, and gestures. Just like a human friend (or maybe even better!), a companion animal will look into your eyes to assess your emotional state and attempt to understand what you're thinking and feeling and respond in a calming and soothing manner. In doing so, companion animals help reduce and manage stress, anxiety, depression, and ease loneliness. But what exactly takes place when we interact with a companion animal that makes us feel so good? Researchers speculate that the levels of oxytocin (the "love" or "cuddle" hormone that is released when people snuggle up or bond socially) often increases, as does the production of the feel-good brain chemical called "serotonin." A research study at Azabu University in Japan showed that oxytocin levels rose significantly when owners and dogs gazed at each other and profoundly affected both owners **and** their dogs. Of the dyad that spent most of the time looking into each other's eyes, dogs experienced a 130% rise in oxytocin levels, and owners experienced a 300% increase! This supports the existence of a self-perpetuating oxytocin-mediated positive feedback loop in human-dog relationships that is similar to that of human mother-infant relations. In other words, our love grows with our canine companions the longer we spend with them. Is it any surprise that we grieve so deeply when this bond is broken through death or other permanent separation?

Real Life Vignettes of the Mental and Physical Health Benefits of the Human-Animal Bond.

The following are real-life narratives taken from clinical, research, and book interviews that speak to the human-animal bond's mental and physical health benefits. These are just a few examples of how grieving pet owners describe their experience of deep and profound connection, and perhaps you might find validation, hope, and connection through these brief vignettes.

Julianne C. and Canine Companion Bridgit:

The way in which Bridgit and I were a mirror to each other's lives was truly a blessing and a miracle; I'm guessing for both of us. Together we endured physical sufferings and surgeries, many of which occurred in parallel or succession to each other. From brain surgeries to Lyme treatment, we went through it all together; whether enduring or recovering Bridgit was always close by my side. She was my emotional support during the psychological difficulty's secondary to disruptions in my physical health. Bridgit showed me, by example, how to never EVER give up hope. She showed me that perfection was nothing more than an unattainable ideal, and the beauty in imperfection was certainly worth opening my eyes to. Because of her, I recovered with passion, and because of me, she recovered with the certainty of yet one more day on the horizon; always one more day until the end. Bridgit was my lifeline during my darkest and painful days of physical challenges. But she kept me in the game; always kept me in the game no matter how far away I was. During those difficult days, hope and Bridgit were my lifeline to mental and physical health. My sweet, beautiful Bridgit was and will always be my wellspring of health, vitality, and hope.

Susan G. and Canine Companion Star:

I am a recent widower with no human children, and most of my friends are deceased, and my family does not live close. Shortly after my husband passed, I became very depressed, lonely, and began isolating myself. With the encouragement of a thoughtful neighbor, I ended up rescuing a dog; or should I say he recused me? Star is my first dog and I really had no idea what to expect. However, since Star came into my life I am not as depressed; I have been getting out more and meeting other pet parents. I'm isolating less and have even been able to come off of my antidepressants. He gives my life meaning and purpose and forces me to get out of my own head and out of my house. It feels good to be responsible to and for something other than myself, as I used to take care of my husband for many years. I feel like we are a family, and while I still struggle with grieving and missing my husband terribly, having Star in my life has been the lifesaver I needed! He is a happy pill in the form of a 15 lb. dog. He changed my life in the most profound way and put a ray of sunshine back where it desperately needed to be.

Erin G. and Canine Companion Sparky:

Before Sparky came into my life, I was a physical and emotional mess. I did not take good care of my physical or mental health. I never thought a dog could have such a significant and positive impact on my life, but he did. After Sparky came into my life, I lost close to 100 lbs. and was able to get off of a lot of medications that I needed due to my unhealthy lifestyle. Sparky put the "spark" back in my life and made me happy, content and showed me how to have fun again. He was the driving force behind our daily walks which started out at just 1/8 of a mile, and eventually, we got up to 6-mile daily hikes and sometimes more on the weekends. I had this little guy that I was responsible for and who gave me such a sense of peace and calm. I felt obligated to give him all the goodness he gave me, so I made sure he had a happy and healthy life. I miss him so dearly, and I still bring his collar and ashes with me on my now solo hikes. I keep his spirit alive by continuing to live the healthy life we created together. RIP my sweet Sparky and thank you for your everlasting gifts.

Sandra and Canine Companion Prince:

I have suffered from Generalized Anxiety Disorder and Panic Disorder for most of my life, which lead to Hypertension. Despite therapy and medication, I had a difficult time managing my symptoms. It was not until Prince came into my life that I experienced a sense of peace and calm for the first time in my life. Prince had a way of calming me and soothing me better than any pill ever could. He was my Emotional Support Animal and instinctively knew when I was having a bad day, and when my anxiety was spiking. His mellow and loving presence had such a powerful impact on me that I began having less panic attacks and my blood pressure was controlled, for the first time in decades, without medication. He had such a powerful and long-lasting impact on both my emotional and physical health; even though he is no longer with me, those are his gifts to me that are everlasting. I miss my buddy Prince beyond words...

> *"The vulnerability present in the smallest of God's creatures calls out to our noblest instincts."*
> *– Monks of New Skete*

CHAPTER TWO:

Our Special Bond: Eternal Memories

Reflecting on your bond throughout the years allows you to remember the positive aspects and memories of your beloved companion animal; not just the pain of grieving.

Additionally, people often fear the memories of everyday life with their companion animal will begin to fade over time, so capturing this information while still fresh in your mind can offer an effective way to preserve your memories.

Below are journal questions and prompts to help you reflect on your special time together during the very beginning of your relationship.

Our Bond: The Very Beginning

How and when I first met you and what my feelings, reactions, and first impressions were:

_____

_____

_____

_____

_____

_____

_____

_____

The reason I wanted YOU and /or the reason you were chosen for me:

_____

_____

_____

_____

_____

_____

_____

Your registered name, call name, birthday, and date I brought you home:

_____

_____

_____

_____

Why I chose your name and it's significance:

_____

_____

_____

_____

My memories of how you looked, felt, smelled, etc., when you were a puppy/kitten, etc.:

_____

_____

_____

_____

_____

When reflecting on our beginning together, I can recall your unique and evolving personality as (describe characteristics that were central to your beloved pet):

_____
_____
_____
_____
_____
_____
_____
_____

As a puppy/kitten etc., your favorite activity, food, sleeping spots and, toys were:

_____
_____
_____
_____
_____
_____
_____
_____

As a puppy/kitty etc., a typical morning/day/evening together would go something like this:

_____

_____

_____

_____

_____

_____

_____

Some of our favorite places to visit when you were young were:

_____

_____

_____

_____

_____

_____

_____

_____

Things I learned from you and/or that you taught me about myself during our very beginning together:

_____

_____

_____

_____

_____

_____

_____

My fondest and happiest memories of you as a puppy/kitten etc. are:

_____

_____

_____

_____

_____

_____

_____

_____

_____

_____

When I think of your very early years, the things I miss most are:

_____

_____

_____

_____

_____

_____

_____

Reflecting on you as a puppy/kitten etc. brings about feelings of:

_____

_____

_____

_____

_____

_____

_____

_____

Reflections on Our Bond and Relationship: The Beginning:

"Dogs have a way of finding the people who need them and filling an emptiness we didn't even know we had."

– Thom Jones

Below are journal questions and prompts to help you reflect on your special time together during the adolescent years.

Our Bond: Your Adolescent Years

How our bond together grew in your adolescent years; circumstances, challenges, that brought us closer together:

_____

_____

_____

_____

_____

_____

_____

_____

_____

_____

_____

_____

_____

_____

_____

_____

_____

_____

_____

The special activities we did together in your adolescent years that further cultivated our bond:

_____

_____

_____

_____

_____

_____

As your distinctive personality began to unfold, you were appointed many nicknames. Some of my favorite nicknames for you and how they came about:

_____

_____

_____

_____

_____

_____

_____

_____

My memories of how you looked in your adolescent years:

_____

_____

_____

_____

_____

_____

_____

When reflecting on your adolescent years, this is how I recall your unique and evolving personality as (describe characteristics that were central to your beloved pet):

_____

_____

_____

_____

_____

_____

_____

_____

_____

In your adolescent years, your favorite food, sleeping spot, and toys were:

_____

_____

_____

_____

_____

_____

In your adolescent years, a typical morning/
afternoon/evening together would look something like
this:

_____

_____

_____

_____

_____

_____

_____

In your adolescent years, some of your favorite activities and places to visit were:

_____

_____

_____

_____

_____

_____

_____

_____

Things I learned from you and/or that you taught me about myself in your adolescent years:

_____

_____

_____

_____

_____

_____

_____

_____

_____

What I miss most about our time together during your adolescent years and my happiest memories of you:

_____

_____

_____

_____

_____

_____

How you would greet me when I returned home after being away:

_____

_____

_____

_____

_____

_____

_____

Thinking about your adolescent years brings about feelings of:

Reflections on Our Bond and Relationship: Your Adolescent Years

> *"If having a soul means being able to feel love and loyalty and gratitude, then animals are better off than a lot of humans."*
> *- James Herriot*

Below are journal questions and prompts to help you reflect on your special time together during the adult years.

Our Bond: Your Adult Years

How our bond together continued to mature in your adult years; circumstances, challenges, events that brought us closer together:

_____

_____

_____

_____

_____

_____

_____

_____

_____

_____

_____

_____

_____

_____

_____

The special activities we did together in your adult years that further cultivated our maturing bond:

How we would celebrate birthdays, holidays, and special events:

My memories of how you looked in your adult years:

_____

_____

_____

_____

_____

_____

_____

When reflecting on your adult years, this is how I recall your unique and evolving personality (describe characteristics that were central to your beloved pet):

_____

_____

_____

_____

_____

_____

_____

_____

In your adult years, your favorite activities and places to visit:

In your adult years, your favorite food, sleeping spots, and toys were:

In your adult years, a typical morning/afternoon/evening together would look something like this:

_____

_____

_____

_____

_____

_____

_____

Things I learned from you and/or that you taught me about myself in your adult years:

_____

_____

_____

_____

_____

_____

_____

What I miss most about our time together during your adult years:

_____

_____

_____

_____

_____

_____

_____

My fondest and happiest memories as an adult are:

_____

_____

_____

_____

_____

_____

_____

_____

Reflecting on your adult years brings about feeling of:

Reflections on Our Bond and Relationship: Your Adult Years:

"He is your friend, your partner, your defender, your dog. You are his life, his love, his leader. He will be yours faithful and true to the last beat of his heart. You owe it to him to be worthy of such devotion."

- Anonymous

Below are journal questions and prompts to help you reflect on your special time together during your senior years.

Our Bond: Your Senior Years

How our bond continued to grow in your senior years; circumstances, challenges, and events that brought us closer together:

_____

_____

_____

_____

_____

_____

_____

_____

_____

_____

_____

_____

_____

_____

_____

_____

_____

_____

Special activities we did together that continued to grow and strengthen our bond in your senior years:

_____

_____

_____

_____

_____

_____

_____

As you continued in your senior years, the subtle and not so subtle changes I noticed:

_____

_____

_____

_____

_____

_____

_____

_____

Ways in which our routine began to change as you grew older:

_____

_____

_____

_____

_____

_____

_____

_____

My memories of how you looked in your senior years:

_____

_____

_____

_____

_____

_____

_____

_____

When reflecting on your senior years, I can recall your unique personality and defining features as (describe characteristics that were central to your beloved pet):

_____

_____

_____

_____

_____

_____

_____

In your senior years, your favorite activity and places to visit:

_____

_____

_____

_____

_____

_____

_____

In your senior years, your favorite food, sleeping spots, and toys were:

_____

_____

_____

_____

_____

_____

_____

In your senior years, a typical morning/afternoon/ evening together would look something like this:

_____

_____

_____

_____

_____

_____

_____

_____

Things I learned from you and /or that you taught me about myself in your senior years:

_____

_____

_____

_____

_____

_____

_____

What I miss most about our time together during your senior years:

_____

_____

_____

_____

_____

_____

_____

_____

_____

My fondest and happiest memories of you in your senior years:

Reflecting on your senior years brings about feeling of:

Reflections on Our Bond and Relationship: Your Senior Years

"As I see your time is near, and the days of your youth have taken flight, every last breath I will spend by your side, I will not leave you to make this journey alone. Our time together seemed to be contained in that one final and last breath...one that I will remember for eternity. I will miss you my dear companion, for eternity I will miss you."

-Julianne Corbin

Below are journal questions and prompts to help you reflect on the final days, weeks, and/or months of your beloved companion animal's life.

The End of Your Life

This is how I remember our final months, weeks, and days together:

_____

_____

_____

_____

_____

_____

_____

_____

_____

_____

_____

_____

_____

_____

_____

_____

_____

_____

Special "last time" events that we shared together and how I felt about them:

How you told me that it was okay and time to go or how I made
that decision for you and what that was like:

The circumstances around your final passage and how I felt and /or continue to feel about it (natural death, planned euthanasia, unexpected, at home, at veterinarian hospital):

_____

_____

_____

_____

_____

_____

_____

_____

_____

_____

_____

_____

_____

_____

_____

_____

_____

_____

The reason I chose to be with you when you died or chose not to be with you and what that was like:

_____

_____

_____

_____

_____

_____

_____

How I felt immediately after you passed:

_____

_____

_____

_____

_____

_____

_____

_____

Why I chose to be with your body after you died or why I chose not to and what it was like:

_____

_____

_____

_____

_____

_____

How I chose to take care of your remains:

_____

_____

_____

_____

_____

_____

_____

_____

Important items of yours that I placed with your body after you died and what they symbolized about you and our relationship:

_____

_____

_____

_____

_____

_____

_____

I did or did not have a memorial service to commemorate your life. If so, this is where it was, what was done and said, and who attended:

_____

_____

_____

_____

_____

_____

_____

_____

_____

Your final resting place and why it was chosen for you:

This is how I chose to take care of your personal items such as your collar, toys, bed, etc.:

Special items of yours that I have chosen to keep forever:

_____

_____

_____

_____

_____

_____

_____

Looking back on the "era" that was you, the role you played in my life, and the needs you fulfilled can be best described as:

_____

_____

_____

_____

_____

_____

_____

_____

_____

Looking back at our time together, the eternal gifts you gave
me are:

_____

_____

_____

_____

_____

_____

This is how you kept me grounded and centered:

_____

_____

_____

_____

_____

_____

_____

_____

Some of the difficult things we went through together and how you helped me:

_____

_____

_____

_____

_____

_____

_____

How I helped you during difficult and challenging times:

_____

_____

_____

_____

_____

_____

_____

_____

_____

The "would of," "should of," "could of" thoughts that go through my mind regarding the end of your life:

_____

_____

_____

_____

_____

_____

_____

Any regrets I have and why:

_____

_____

_____

_____

_____

_____

_____

_____

If I could change the ending of your life, this is how it would look:

I did or did not write a eulogy for you. If not, why? If so, this is what it says:

Reflections on The End of Your Life:

"What we have enjoyed, we can never lose;all that we love deeply becomes a part of us."
- Helen Keller

CHAPTER THREE:

My Healing Journey Through Companion Animal Loss

Companion Animal Loss: An Introduction and FAQ's

For many, the loss of a companion animal remains one of the most disregarded, misunderstood, and painful losses one can experience and only recently taken with the importance it deserves. Our grief is not a disease or illness that needs to be "fixed"; it is a universal and natural emotional reaction to the loss of anything close and meaningful to us, which of course, includes the death of a beloved companion animal. Grief is an on-going emotional, psychological, and spiritual process of healing, changing, adjusting, and adapting, which takes time. In my professional experience working with both pet loss and human loss, it is perfectly normal and expected for grievers to find the first year+ following a significant loss difficult and turbulent. During that first year, you are learning what it means not to have your companion animal by your side as you try to adjust and adapt to a life that no longer includes them; you are attempting to make sense out of the loss and how to move forward in your life. During that first year you will experience a long series of "firsts" such as; holidays, birthdays, anniversaries, and other significant annual events for the first time without your companion animal. Grief is the feeling we have when we reach out for our companion animal who's always been there, only to discover when we need them again, they are no longer there. The loss of a companion animal is not something you go through; it's something that becomes a part of you as you continue through your life. For some, grief can be an isolating process, and for others, it can be a transformative journey. But one thing is for sure; grief is a pain so deep that it cannot always be spoken. It is an aching and longing that we feel deep in our hearts and soul. While everyone experiences grief in their own way, it is common to experience some of the following after the death of a cherished companion animal:

- uncontrolled tears, crying or sobbing

- changes in sleep patterns, such as difficulty falling asleep or too little/too much sleep

- extreme fatigue and lack of energy

- feeling lethargic or apathetic about daily tasks or life in general

- change in appetite; such as loss of appetite, overeating, or emotional eating

- withdrawing from normal or usual social interactions and relationships

- difficulty concentrating or focusing on a task, whether at work, personally, a hobby, etc.

- questioning spiritual or religious beliefs, career choices, or life goals

- feelings of anger, guilt, loneliness, depression, emptiness, sadness, with just occasional moments of joy/happiness

To help understand the grief of losing a companion animal, it is only natural that we look to human loss to help us conceptualize and validate what we are feeling. Many people think about the grief associated with the death of a companion animal as being just like that of a human loved one, and we will find ourselves processing back and forth through a set of "stages" such as;

- Shock and Denial

- Painful Emotions

- Living in the Past

- Acceptance and Reconciliation and

- Continuance

Yet, many grieving pet owners struggle more with losing a companion animal then a human loved one. Why is this? While there is no one simple answer, by looking at the *differences*, not the *similarities* between companion animal loss and human loss, we can begin to understand the difficulties we experience when our companion animals die. While grieving the loss of a companion animal may follow a pattern similar to human loss, published research and real-life experience tells us that there are factors that distinguish these two losses and plays a role in making the death of a companion animal especially difficult to reconcile. Some of the factors that separate companion animal loss from human loss is; our loss and grief are disenfranchised from communal supports as; grieving pet owners we do not have a formal way to memorialize publicly and mourn our loss, and we are forced to say good-bye to many different relationships at the same time. These differences can set the stage for many emotional and psychological difficulties such as; complicated grief reaction, PTSD, depression, and anxiety.

As you engage in your grieving process, remember that grief is just that; it is a process. If you try to squash it down or ignore it, it will inevitably find a way to inform and underscore every aspect of your life. If allowed to have a voice, your grief will follow a progression that is unique to you. We cannot cut tangents with quick fixes or cliques designed to silence the voice of grief. Grief is an expression that links the living to the deceased; a symbolic integration of the very essence of the relationship is a love that knows no boundaries and has no end. Be kind and gentle with yourself and take as much time as you need to mourn and grieve the loss of your beloved companion and family member. Peace to all…

Frequently Asked Questions:

1. **Are there "stages" of companion animal loss, and are they similar to that of human loss?** Yes, there are stages that the bereaved go through after the death of a companion animal that shares characteristics of human loss. Based on my years of clinical work with grieving companion animal owners and as highlighted in my research on the Human-Animal Bond (2006), these stages follow a general non- linear pattern of:

   - **Shock and Disbelief**

   - **Painful Emotions**

   - **Living in the Past**

   - **Acceptance, Reconciliation**

   - **Continuance and Transcendence**

   These stages, which will be discussed in the following chapters, are in no way absolute and serve only as a guide to help you understand your grieving process. It is essential to keep in mind that there is no predetermined timeline for your grieving process; it can be long and difficult with many ebbs and flows along the way. Likewise, grieving is never a linear process; it is natural and expected to move back and forth from one stage to another or to feel a sense of permeability between stages, especially soon after the loss. As touched on earlier, while the stages of pet loss share similarities to that of human loss, variables such as the disenfranchised nature of the loss, the role pets play in our lives, and the relationship' can all have a direct impact on the way we experience our grief.

2. **How long will it take to "get over" the death of my companion animal?** I don't like to use the word "get over" to describe grief; a cold is something we get over, not the death of a beloved companion animal. The reality is you will not 'get over' the loss; you will learn to live with their absence, and you will slowly begin to adjust and adapt to a life without their physical presence. You will heal, and you will rebuild yourself around the loss you have suffered. The time frame for healing and reconciliation varies from individual to individual. Variables such as your companion animal's age, circumstances involving the death, the nature of your bond and relationship, your emotional constitution, and support system all play a role in how long it will take to process your grief. Grief is never a straightforward process, and it is common to move back and forth from one stage to another. While some people may notice their intense grief symptoms lessening in 6-8 months, others take much longer. **Generally** speaking, if your grief symptoms have not decreased in 12 months or at any time you feel suicidal, it is recommended that you seek the help of a trained and licensed mental health professional.

3. **I never thought the death of my pet would be this painful. Is this normal?** I've had many clients share that they felt more grief over the loss of their companion animal than the loss of family members or friends, creating intense feelings of guilt and despair. It is important to remember that it's not **what** you have lost, but rather the **nature and degree** of your attachment, connection, love, and meaning that your companion animal had in your life that defines your grieving process. Despite what others may believe, it is completely normal to feel intense grief after the death of your beloved companion animal. It is important that you find people and resources that will validate your loss and provide comfort.

4. **I know she/he was a companion animal, but I loved them like my own child, and no one seems to understand. Is there something wrong with me?** No, your ability to love so deeply is not "wrong." For certain people, a companion animal can be the "object" by which maternal and paternal impulses and instincts are projected onto, especially those without human children. So yes, your companion animal can take on a similar emotional and psychological role in your life that a child would. It is important to honor that your relationship was extremely deep and meaningful and not judge yourself for the bond you shared with your beloved.

5. **When is the right time to get another pet?** There is no definitive answer to this question. As we all know, and it is important to remember, companion animals are not replaceable or interchangeable. People will often impulsively rush to get another companion animal to avoid the grieving process. This is not only unfair to your new companion since it may not live up to your expectations, but also does

a disservice to you by not allowing yourself space and time to grieve properly. On the other hand, I've had clients who shared that getting a new companion animal was the only thing that helped to heal their hearts and allowed them to move forward. Every person is different, and only you will know when the time is right. I often say to my clients that if you wait till you no longer miss your deceased companion animal, you may never bring another into your life because there will always be a part of you that misses your beloved. Being in the emotional space where you can continue to be present and tend to your grieving process while opening your heart and home to a new family member is when the time may be right.

6. **Can one experience grief when the loss is unrelated to death?** The "loss" of a companion animal can take on many forms, and one needs not die to experience grief. For example, if your companion animal becomes lost or if you are forced to give him or her up due to relocation or declining health are situations that can bring on intense grief. Our lives are filled with many necessary losses that do not include death. Watching our once young and vibrant companion animal grow old reminds us that (most likely) we will outlive them, and this can trigger emotional distress and anticipatory grief. It is challenging to watch someone we love grow old, and while this is the natural course of life, it can trigger our own issues surrounding death, dying, and mortality.

7. **What is "anticipatory grief," and how is it relevant to the death of a companion animal?** Grieving is not something that only happens *after* our beloved companion animals die. Still, the grieving process can begin much sooner for those tending to the aging or terminally ill. Emotionally

preparing for our companion's end of life is what defines anticipatory grief. While anticipatory grief shares commonalities with grief experienced after the loss of a loved one, some symptoms unique to anticipatory grief are:

- feelings of rapid cycling depression

- rehearsal of the details of your companion animal's final moments and end of life

- attempts minimize the consequences of your companion's end of life

- increased anxiety, worry, and irritability

- mourning the changes in your companion animal's personality or physical appearance

Anticipatory grief can often be mixed in with the hope that your pet will live longer or survive their terminal illness, while grief after the loss mourns a loss that has already occurred. As our once young and vibrant companion animals grow old or become ill, we are forced to acknowledge the impermanence of all living things. It is in this space of anticipation that we may begin to mourn our loss.

"The reality is that you will grieve forever. You will not 'get over' the loss of a loved one; you will learn to live with it. You will heal, and you will rebuild yourself around the loss you have suffered. You will be whole again, but you will never be the same."

-Elisabeth Kubler-Ross

General Pet Bereavement Journal Prompts

Sometimes it's hard to know where to begin the process of journaling because our feelings associated with loss are not always clear, and we do not know exactly where or how to start. Following are some general prompts and questions that I use as a starting point to help my clients get in touch with their feelings of grief and loss. Some prompts are general, and some more specific. You may find you resonate with some questions more than others, so focus on the questions that seem most important and meaningful to you. Remember, there is no "right" or "wrong" way to journal!

I remember when....

_____

_____

_____

_____

_____

_____

_____

_____

_____

The first time I _____and what that was like for me:

_____

_____

_____

_____

_____

_____

_____

_____

_____

What I recall and felt in those first hours and days after you died:

_____
_____
_____
_____
_____
_____
_____
_____
_____
_____

What I recall and felt in the first weeks after you died:

_____
_____
_____
_____
_____
_____
_____
_____
_____
_____
_____

If applicable, what I recall and felt on the first anniversary of your death:

The most difficult lessons I have learned since your passing are:

The greatest lesson I have learned since your passing is:

How I felt the first time I visited one of our favorite places:

Some healthy and not so healthy ways I express my grief:

Some of the ways that I hold in my grief:

How I would describe my grieving process thus far:

_____

_____

_____

_____

_____

_____

_____

Words that best describe how I feel today:

_____

_____

_____

_____

_____

_____

_____

_____

_____

How it felt on first anniversary dates such as your birthday, holidays, change of seasons, etc.:

_____

_____

_____

_____

_____

_____

_____

_____

My happiest memory of you is and why:

_____

_____

_____

_____

_____

_____

_____

_____

_____

This is what I want or need to say to you:

_____

_____

_____

_____

_____

_____

_____

_____

_____

_____

_____

_____

_____

_____

_____

_____

_____

_____

_____

_____

Additional Reflections:

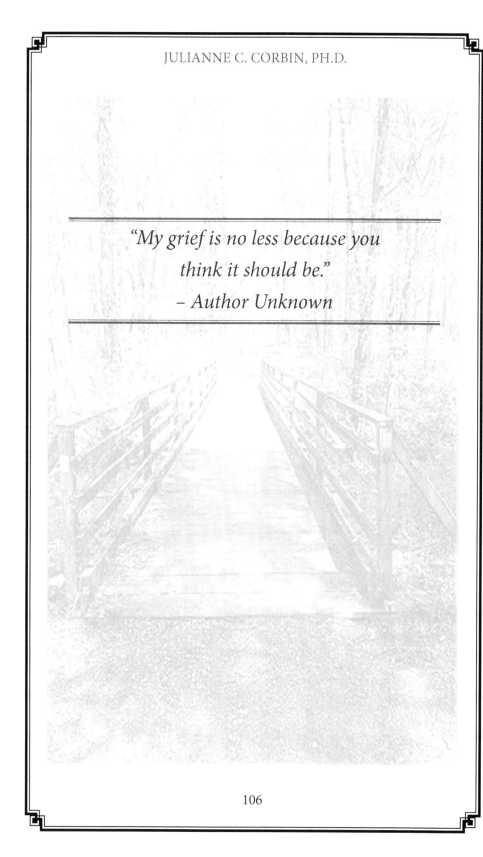

"*My grief is no less because you think it should be.*"
– *Author Unknown*

Companion Animal Loss and Disenfranchised Grief

Having worked with both human loss and companion animal loss, I have seen a great divide in who gets to own the greatest loss ever. Is it the death of a spouse, sibling, child, friend, or companion animal? I have worked with clients who have lost children and spouses. I have worked with grown men who have lost family members and claim to never have cried a single tear in their lives, only to break down into a thousand pieces after the death of a cherished companion animal. Over my 20 years of working with grieving clients what I have learned is that the most difficult loss is the one you are currently experiencing, and no one has the right to judge its net worth. While there are some differences between human loss and companion animal loss, generally speaking, the grieving process is the same. However, every loss is different for each individual, with many variables setting the stage for the process that follows. In attempts to understand why the death of a companion animal can be one of the most difficult losses for many people, we must not only consider the nature of the relationship and depth of the bond as discussed earlier but also how the disenfranchised nature of the loss contributes to the inherent difficulties. The grief is real, and the grief is life-changing. For many, one's grief is latent with guilt for feeling such intense sadness over the death of a "pet."

Disenfranchised grief is any grief that is not acknowledged as significant and the type of grief experienced when a loss cannot be openly acknowledged, socially sanctioned, or publicly mourned. Disenfranchised Grief generally falls into one (or sometimes more) of the following categories:

1. The loss is not seen as worthy of grief (non-death losses, companion animal loss)

2. The relationship is stigmatized (civil marriages, same-sex partners, companion animal bonds)

3. The mechanism of death is stigmatized (suicide or over-dose death)

4. The person grieving is not recognized as a griever (co-workers, ex-partners, pet owners)

5. The way someone is grieving is stigmatized. (ex. the absence of an outward grief response or extreme grief responses)

Examples of Disenfranchised Grief can include situations related or unrelated to death, such as:

- loss of fertility/infertility
- financial loss/loss of job
- chronic and debilitating medical conditions/loss of health
- estrangement from family
- grieving those missing in military
- grieving missing children or adults
- loss of independence
- divorce
- death by suicide
- death of a sibling
- death of an unmarried partner
- death of a beloved companion animal

When we lose a dearly loved companion animal, our grief becomes disenfranchised. The relationship and loss are minimized and not recognized by society as significant enough to warrant grieving. There is a false assumption that closeness and love can exist and thrive only between humans, but as a collective group of companion animal lovers, we know this could not be further from the truth! People who do not understand the unique bond between a human and companion animal fail to recognize the emotional, psychological, and spiritual bonding that occurs and the implications when those bonds are broken through death or other finalities. Those suffering the loss of a cherished companion animal often suffer alone and in isolation, are marginalized from social supports commonly available after the death of a human loved one, and have fewer opportunities to express and resolve their grief. This alienation experience from community support and resources sets the stage for a host of emotional and psychological symptoms associated with prolonged or complicated grief. For example, in my research, *A Phenomenological Study of Canine Loss and Grief Response: Clinical and Depth Psychological Implications (2006)*, 95% of participants as well as a significant number of grieving clients in my psychotherapy practice met the criteria for disenfranchised loss and complicated grief response. Below are some important points to think about regarding the disenfranchised nature of companion animal loss that may help you to understand why your grieving experience is incredibly challenging:

- The *relationship and bond* between humans and companion animal is not always acknowledged and recognized by society as relevant or significant enough to warrant grief. We have all heard the hurtful and insensitive statements, "it was just a dog or cat" or "just get another one" in response to the loss of our cherished family member. These statements can make us feel as though our relationship was insignificant. Family and friends' failure to understand the relationship's significance leads to marginalizing and isolating you from psychological supports typically available after a human loss. This lack of understanding and recognition of the relationship and bond we share with our companion animals can have an insurmountable impact on our emotional healing process.

- The *loss* of a companion animal is not always regarded as worthy of grieving and is consequently minimized by others. The lack of empathy and validation from others can lead to feelings of embarrassment about expressing grief, resulting in the bereaved suppressing their emotions and engaging in isolating and maladaptive behaviors as a way to cope. Considering the lack of understanding from society surrounding the significance of companion animal loss, there are fewer opportunities to openly express and resolve one's feelings with friends, family, and the community. This serves to alienate those grieving the loss of a companion animal from community resources, social interactions, and emotional support.

- *There is no formal way to memorializing or opportunity to publicly mourn the loss of a beloved companion animal.* Memorializing is a critical component to our grieving process, but many grieving pet owners do not engage in memorial services typical after a human loss. A funeral and memorial service offers the opportunity for us to;

- express affection and gratitude to our beloved companion animals

- receive emotional support, sympathy, and comfort

- express and share our sorrow and talk about our loss

- concretize and accept the reality of our loss

- assists in facilitating our grieving process.

After the death of our companion animal, the healing aspects of memorializing noted above are not available, and this has severe consequences on our ability to accept the finality of the death, further marginalizing us and creates a sense of isolation and aloneness that may not be experienced during human loss. For additional information on memorializing your companion animal, please see Chapter Three.

Companion Animal Loss and Disenfranchised Grief
Therapeutic Journaling Questions

For those who have been fortunate enough not to experience the disenfranchised aspect of companion animal loss, the following journal questions may not be relevant. For others, the following questions and reflections help guide you towards re-enfranchising your loss by identifying and expressing your feelings about your experience of disenfranchised loss and will help you gain a deeper understanding of how the marginalized loss of your beloved pet has informed your grieving process. Reflecting on these questions will help validate your loss by recognizing that your loss and associated feelings are normal, relevant, and important!

Since you died, I find that sometimes (or all the time!) I feel as if I do not have the right or am not entitled to grieve. The reasons that I feel this way and how this makes me feel...

Since you died, I feel like there is something wrong with me because of how deeply I miss you. I feel this way because...

_____

_____

_____

_____

_____

Knowing that my pain reflects how much I love and miss you; I will begin to honor you and our relationship by:

_____

_____

_____

_____

_____

_____

_____

Regardless of how others have supported or not supported me, I must actively acknowledge that my love for you is real, significant, and your loss no less valid than human loss (s). Some mantra's and supportive statements that I can repeat to myself in difficult times are:

Although I feel very alone at times, perhaps if I look around me, there are supports in places I have never thought of. Some of these places or people might be:

_____

_____

_____

_____

_____

_____

_____

Even though I wanted to, or it was too difficult, I felt that it was not "acceptable" for me to engage in a ritual or memorial to honor your life and passing. Knowing it IS healthy and natural, this is how I can see having a memorial in your honor:

_____

_____

_____

_____

_____

_____

_____

Knowing that my grief is a testament to my love and devotion to you, I give myself permission to explore my grief and express my emotions in a way unique to our relationship and personal to me. Some ways that I can see doing this are:

Sometimes I feel as though your death is not worthy of time and space to grieve. I feel this way because:

_____

_____

_____

_____

_____

_____

I must actively and mindfully remind myself that I am worthy of grieving and that my grief is important. I give myself permission to grieve. Ways that I can be mindful of my mourning process are:

_____

_____

_____

_____

_____

_____

_____

Additional Reflections on Disenfranchised Grief

Real Life Vignettes of Companion Animal Loss and Disenfranchised Grief

Following are real-life narratives taken from clinical, research, and book interviews that highlight Companion Animal Loss and Disenfranchised Grief. These are just a few examples of how grieving pet owners describe their experience, and perhaps you might find validation, hope, and connection through these brief stories.

Joyce C. and Canine Companion Toby:

There are just so many things to say, but the thing that really impacts my grieving process is that I feel embarrassment about the whole thing. It's as if my circle of friends, family, and co-workers really do not understand how Toby's death has impacted me. They make me feel like there is something wrong with me for grieving over Toby's death. I eventually decided not to show my feelings because I am embarrassed by my display of emotions. My family and circle of friends' message is that a dog is not worth crying over or grieving over. They would say things like "just get another one" or" pull yourself together, "it was just a dog," and it really hurts my feelings. I thought it would be healthy for me to express my sadness but doing so only makes it worse. So, I either feel self-conscious and embarrassed by my reaction or keep it to myself and feel like I am going to implode. I don't have the understanding and support you get when a human loved one dies, and it makes it so much harder; I feel like I am an island onto myself. People just don't understand, but they should be there for me instead of judging me if they really cared about me. It has been a real eye-opening experience for me.

Marsha L. and Canine Companion Chauncey:

I feel a lot of shame as if I am not entitled to my grief. Why? Because Chauncey was a dog? I am so bitter about how my friends, family, and society, in general, have reacted to my loss. Something horrible happened to my family; My beautiful 15 yr. old niece was killed in a car accident a few years back, and it was just horrific for all of us, just horrible. During that time, Chauncey is what kept me together; without him, I think I would have lost it. Anyway, there was the funeral, the flowers, the viewing, the support, the cards, the outpouring of love and support, etc. You know all the things you would expect when something like that happens. I was there for my brother and sister-in-law for pretty much anything they needed. That was about five years ago. When Chauncey died, there were none of those things, none. There was no funeral, no viewing, no way of paying respect and saying good-bye, no cards, no flowers, no real support. I was expected to drop a few tears and be okay in a few days. I was so filled with anger and hurt and then later shame. I made a point to let everyone know how bad I was hurting and how he really was my son, the only "child" I ever had. For me, it was like losing my child, and I just remember not getting a single card or anything from people who were supposed to care about me. The first time I saw my sister-in-law after Chauncey died, she did not even ask how I was doing. It was life as usual for everyone, that is everyone but me. I still feel some shame as if there is something wrong with me for hurting so much.

Meghan E. and Canine Companion Kay:

The hardest part for me was/is the lack of understanding and support. How many times do I have to hear that she was just a dog or just get another? These things are so hurtful. The one thing that still stands out for me is that after Kay died, I could not take any bereavement days off from work; apparently, that is not policy, however, my co-worker's great-grandmother died whom she never even met, and she got days off for bereavement. At work, I could not hold it together and I would just have to run to the bathroom and cry. I felt so alone and also ashamed of my feelings. The message I was getting was that it is not normal to grieve the loss of an animal and just to move on. This was when I got even more sad and depressed. I had no one to share my pain with. It was me and my antidepressants, and that was it. It was such a dark time in my life, and I am still so bitter by the lack of support I received. What stands out for me is the lack of support and how that made it even more difficult for me emotionally.

Janet T. and Canine Companion Cassie:

Cassie was euthanized at the hospital, and the reaction of the staff was cold and heartless. It was as if it was just another day at the office; like, okay, she is dead, and don't forget to pay at the front desk on your way out. I got no comfort from them at all. No one seemed to understand how painful this was for me. No one showed any real support. Cassie was like my child, no more than a child; she was my best friend and confidante of 13 years. She was a part of my life, every part of my life for 13 years, and no one respected or cared to understand the impact on me. I am still so angry that I could not share my grief with anyone. Early on, people would ask what happened and when I would tell them Cassie died and they would look at me like I was crazy and say some very mean comments that just hurt so bad. If Mary Jane, down the street, lost her child to cancer, do you think people would react to her that way? Of course not, but because Cassie was a dog, I was not supposed to grieve. So, I hide my pain and try to carry on as if all was normal. Not having anyone to talk to, not receiving any validation for my pain was so hard. I am already an outcast because I am not married and do not have human children. I just never knew someone could feel so alone. Even my Psychologist acted as if I should not be grieving as I was because, in his words, "she was not your human child." Can you imagine someone trained to understand and know these things was acting just like everyone else? The whole part of not being understood, not feeling entitled to my grief, and not having any support from my friends, family, or society was devastating.

Callie T. and Canine Companion Psalms:

People have minimized and downplayed my pain and my grief. They were concerned for about one week, and afterward, the telephone calls and support just stopped. The Veterinarian office was concerned while she was alive, but after she passed, there was nothing. I received cards in the mail but nothing else. It felt like Psalms was just a patient that equaled money and their money make was gone. My holistic vet called me on the phone and also hugged me. I appreciate her telephone call the most because she was sincere. My family does not understand. They would say, yes, we all loved her, but death is natural. Knowing death is natural did not help me feel better; it made me feel like I was not entitled to my grief. For a while, I would cry all the time and anywhere. People's comfort level with my sadness decreased over time, so while my crying has not necessarily stopped, I cry in private now or go somewhere secluded (i.e., bathroom). I have mastered stopping tears before the fall.

Marcie S. and Canine Companion Shayna:

When I lost Shayna, I definitely felt isolated for a long time. I literally felt as if no one understood the impact her death had on me. Even as much as my husband loved her and helped care for her, she was my dog for 6 or 7 years before I met him. He wasn't impacted by her death like I was, nor would I expect him to be. I felt destroyed and devastated; like losing a human loved one or maybe even worse. Shayna was like my child and losing her was such a huge loss. Logically you know they're not going to live forever, but when they die, it's literally gut-wrenching pain. I would come home from work every day and sob, look at pictures of her, read poems, watch dog videos on the computer, etc. I felt like nobody really understood, and that made me feel alone and isolated. I think most people just don't place value on a pet's life as they do human life. But the loss can be just as, if not more, significant. I received a few sympathy cards, which I truly appreciated, and her primary Vet sent me a hand-written note and made a donation in her memory. I was still so devastated that I was afraid to tell neighbors because I didn't trust my fragile emotions, so I tried to avoid people for a while for fear of sobbing. I was also single for the majority of my (and her) life, so it was just me and my girl which I think made it more difficult as well. I felt solely responsible for her and began questioning myself; Had I done everything I could do to give her the best life? Had I done everything possible to give her the best medical care? Had I made all the correct decisions in the end? What could I have done differently, and would it have changed the outcome if only for a few days/weeks? Would I have been selfish to try and prolong her life? You may know logically that you're being merciful, but I felt like a "murderer." I had never had to euthanize a dog before, and it was literally one of the most horrible things to go through. These were the kind of thoughts that plagued me for months and months and the reason I finally sought professional counseling. I knew I needed help.

Companion Animal Loss and Complicated Grief

It is important to understand that grief is not a single emotion; it is a state-of-being that impacts us physically, emotionally, psychologically, and spiritually. Each of us is unique in how we experience and process our grief, how long we grieve, and vary considerably from one person to another, even following similar losses, such as in the death of a companion animal. That said, even though everyone experiences grief in a different way, there is a distinction between normal, uncomplicated grief and abnormal, complicated, grief. Grief is a perfectly natural and normal reaction to the loss of someone we love, yet some people find it difficult to reconcile and re-engage in their lives again despite the passage of time and attempts to mourn the loss. Clinically speaking, complicated grief (CG) is "a persistent and on-going form of intense grief in which maladaptive thoughts and dysfunctional behaviors are present along with continued yearning, longing, sadness, and preoccupation with thoughts and memories of the deceased that continues well beyond what is considered "normal and expected." In the case of complicated grief, the bereaved remains in a constant state of intense grief without any progression of the mourning process towards reconciliation and acceptance, and their grief is much more intensified than what you would experience in normal grief. While most people go through several grieving stages after losing a loved one, you may have difficulty reconciling and accepting the loss for years to come with complicated grief. The grief will continue to inform and dominate every aspect of your life. Symptoms common to normal grief diminish over time, with brief episodes triggered by anniversaries, birthdays, holidays, and sensory reminders. The bereaved is aware of the reality of the death but can still perform day-to-day tasks. This is not so for someone experiencing complicated grief; they do not get better over time, and their symptoms become worse and linger. In real-life circumstances, there is no specific amount of time that defines when "normal" grief becomes "complicated grief," however, the Diagnostic Statistical Manual of Mental Disorders (DSM-5) defines six months after the death of a loved one as the time when those grieving should be functioning at "normal" capacity again. Six months, that's all the time you get, and you should be good to go? How can you be expected to reconcile the death of a loved one in just six short months? The truth is we cannot and should not expect ourselves to be back to "normal" in six months or even a year; things may never be as they once were, but you will find and create a new way of being and a new normal.

If you exhibit some of the characteristics of complicated grief listed below, still feel "trapped" in your grief, or find your grief remains the same or continues to intensify over time, then you might consider seeking help from a licensed mental health professional specializing in pet loss. Some characteristics of complicated grief include:

- An inability to focus on anything but the death of your companion animal.

- Focusing intensely on reminders of the deceased or an excessive avoidance of such reminders.

- Irreconcilable feelings of sadness, pain, detachment, sorrow, hopelessness, emptiness, low self-esteem, guilt, or bitterness.

- Problems accepting the finality and reality of the death even after a long period of time.

- Self-destructive/maladaptive behaviors, such as alcohol or drug abuse.

- Suicidal thoughts or actions; If you're experiencing suicidal thoughts, call the National Suicide Prevention Lifeline at 800-273-8255 to speak with a mental health professional.

- Fear the event/trauma will be repeated and hypervigilance towards the circumstances that caused the death.

- Irrational thoughts that the deceased might reappear.

- Intense grief pangs by minor events.

- Preoccupation with thoughts and intrusive images of your animal dying.

- Extreme reactions to anniversaries that do not lessen but may get worse over time.

- Difficulty carrying out normal daily activities and routines.

- Withdrawal from social activities and isolating behaviors.

Now that we know what complicated grief is let's take a brief look at why you, the grieving pet owner, may be at risk. Three important factors give rise to the occurrence of complicated grief in regard to companion animal loss; the loss is disenfranchised and marginalized from society, the painful decision and act of euthanasia, and the multifaceted bond we share. As touched on in the previous chapter, the death and process of grieving a beloved companion animal is disenfranchised from our society and not held with serious intention. The grief that you feel is often disregarded as being trivial and insignificant. You may find yourself removed and marginalized from universal supports typically available after human loss (such as the opportunity to pay tribute to and formally memorialize your companion animal). We know that grieving people who experience disenfranchised losses are more likely to experience complicated grief and grieving pet owners are no exception. The lack of support and validation that grieving pet owners are denied has severe consequences on the healing process and understandably puts this group at risk for prolonged grieving and complicated grief.

In the circumstances involving euthanasia, we are asked to do the impossible; everything we have done to sustain and keep our companion animals alive, safe, and comfortable becomes the very thing we need to cast aside for that final act of love. Understandably so, this final act of love is by far the hardest decision we will ever have to make regarding our companion animal. This final act of love can be extremely traumatizing for those grieving and challenging to come to a place of peace with. Despite guidance and reassurance from veterinary professionals, it is common to become stuck in your process due to overwhelming guilt associated with euthanizing and questioning whether or not the right decision was made at the right time. It should be no surprise that the shock and trauma of euthanizing our companion animals is one of the leading causes of prolonged or complicated grief.

The enriching and sacred bond we share with our companion animals may be like no other relationship in our lives. When they are no longer by our side, we are saying good goodbye to many different relationships at the same time. There are certain dynamics of the bond and relationship that may put the grieving at high risk for experiencing complicated grief after the death of a companion animal such as:

- the degree of attachment and nature of the bond
- the circumstances surrounding the death (euthanasia, unexpected, traumatic, off the timeline, etc.)
- the companion animal having helped the grieving through difficult times and life transitions
- rescuing the companion animal from death or near-death
- having invested extensive time, effort, or financial resources towards medical and health care

- having relied on the companion animal as the main source of support

- experiencing the companion animals as a symbolic link to significant people who are no longer in their lives

I have found a positive correlation between grieving pet owners and Complicated Grief in my research and psychotherapy practice. Ninety percent of clients who presented for pet bereavement counseling scored high on the Inventory of Complicated Grief (ICG) and met the diagnostic criteria. In comparison, only fifty percent of clients presented for bereavement counseling related to human loss scored high on the Inventory of Complicated Grief (ICG) and met the diagnostic criteria. This validates what we already know; that some grieving pet owners are at risk for complicated grief response and other psychological concerns. While my clinical practice does not serve as a research study, it does confirm the findings of my and other published research on canine loss, which illustrates that the loss of a companion animal can be more difficult than human loss, puts the grieving at an increased risk for complicated grief response, PTSD, clinical depression and other psychological struggles. Although there is a collective shift in our culture regarding increased awareness and sensitivity to the grieving process associated with the death of a companion animal, there is still much work to be done. With continued research, clinical, and outreach efforts, we will continue to bring attention to this overlooked and undervalued loss and develop more effective evidence- based treatment for those struggling to cope with the loss of a beloved companion animal. It is important to remember that *the loss of your companion animal is real, the grief you feel is real, and the trauma can be overwhelming, complicated, and prolonged.*

Real Life Vignettes of Companion Animal Loss and Complicated Grief

Following are real-life narratives taken from clinical, research, and book interviews that highlight Companion Animal Loss and Complicated Grief. These are just a few examples of how grieving pet owners describe their experience, and perhaps you might find validation, hope, and connection through these brief stories.

Virginia and Canine Companion Bella:

After Bella passed away, I was going through what I thought was normal grieving, but six months after she passed, I was not moving at all through my process and the depression was a constant and a paralyzing force in my life. I was despondent not just about Bella, but my depression echoed to every aspect of my life. I stopped going to my reading group and stopped going to the gym; I lost a lot of weight and would just sit in silence for hours on end. I even thought of suicide, and in some ways, that felt comforting to me; it was at the moment that I knew this was not normal grief and that something was terribly wrong. I sought therapy and short-term medication, which helped me so much. I found that the better I started to feel, the more I could actually process my grief. Don't be afraid to reach out for help!

Timothy and Canine Companion Lady:

After Lady died, I knew it was normal to feel a lot of different emotions and to feel sad and depressed. I knew that as time went on, I should eventually be able to adjust and accept her being gone. This did not happen for me. Every day for one year my depression and became worse and worse with no end in sight. I was not able to function; lost my job, isolated, and began drinking as a way to cope. It was as though there was a lead weight on me and I could not function; I could not breathe. I was not progressing through any "stages"; even after a year. Lady was my everything, and I did not know how to go on without her, and finally, after a year, I knew what I was feeling was not normal and not healthy. With the help of therapy and sobriety, I came out of my dark space and began to get perspective on my loss. I'm much better now, but I was stuck in a very bad place for a long time.

Diane and Feline Companion Oscar:

Oscar was like a therapy cat to me and helped me managed some emotional struggles I have, so when he died, it unraveled me on many different levels. After he died, I went through what I think was a normal progression of grief early on but then about nine months after he passed away, I began getting worse. My sadness and depression became global and impacted every aspect of my life; I was isolating more, not taking good care of my physical or emotional health and had no hope for my future. It's hard to de-scribe, but if felt different than normal grief, which of course is terribly difficult as well. All of my grief symptoms continued to get more intense and prolonged, even after a year. I was not adjusting at all and almost stopped living altogether. Friends and family no-ticed and helped me to seek treatment, which I am so thankful for. I am grateful that there are professionals that understand this and know how to help. I am still grieving, but I do not feel like I am in quicksand...I feel like there is movement in my process towards some version of healing.

Kenny and Canine Companion Teddy:

The way in which my sweet Teddy died was very traumatizing and made my grieving even more difficult, if not unmanageable. I suffered from severe PTSD symptoms after his death and had uncontrollable flashbacks of his death that were triggered by many things, but mostly, being in my bedroom would trigger a flashback and lead to a full-blown panic attack. Looking back, the PTSD prevented me from really grieving and just caused me to have debilitating symptoms leading to panic attacks. I could not properly mourn Teddy during the first year or so because of this, and my world was just falling apart. I had to take time off from work and began engaging in unhealthy things to cope with my PTSD and loss. I knew I needed help and eventually reached out. I am much better now, and my symptoms are manageable, and I am even able to talk more openly about what happened to Teddy and my grief. I think people need to understand that losing a companion animal can lead to some very debilitating and complicated symptoms. Never minimize the impact of your loss!

> *"Life only demands from you the strength you possess. Only one feat is possible – not to have run away."*
> *-Dag Hammarskjold*

Your Healing Journey: Stages of Companion Animal Loss

In my work as a psychotherapist, grief counselor, and researcher, many grieving pet owners have shared that the loss of their companion animal was one of the most difficult losses they have ever experienced. Many have shared feeling guilt or shame because of the depth and intensity of their grief; however, it is important to understand that your reaction to the loss of your companion animal is **normal and expected.** As discussed in previous chapters, the stages of grief following the loss of a companion animal share many of the same aspects as seen in a human loss but with some notable distinctions. In the pages that follow, you will find stages of grief commonly experienced after the death of a companion animal. This four-stage model of companion animal loss was developed from findings derived from my academic research on the Human-Canine Bond and Pet Loss (2006) and clinical work. These stages are in no way definitive and are intended to provide a general guide and frame of reference for your experience. As you probably already know, the grieving process is not a one-size-fits-all, does not unfold in a linear or predictable manner, and everyone will process through the loss in their own way and in their own time. While it is common to think of grieving in terms of "stages," it can be more like a roller coaster ride, full of ups and downs, highs and lows, and many unexpected stops and starts. Like many roller coasters, the ride tends to be rougher in the beginning, and the lows may be deeper, longer, and more painful. The more difficult periods should become less intense and less frequent as time goes by and you actively work through your process, but it takes time, a lot of time to come to a place of peace, reconciliation, and continuance. Even years after your loss, you may find yourself experiencing moments of intense grief that can take you by surprise. As you process through your healing, remember that grief is not a disease or disorder that needs or can be fixed. The loss of your companion animal is not something that you "get over"; it is something you learn to live with and something you learn to adjust and adapt to. Grief is not a passive event; it is an active emotional, physical, and spiritual state that requires you to actively mourn and be present to. Yes, you may always miss your beloved companion animals, and no amount of time will ever change that reality. What does change over time is how you engage with and experience your grief. If, like so many others, you find yourself questioning your reaction or judging yourself for how intense you are grieving, know that you are not alone, and many others are walking or have walked the same path as you! I hope that the information, tips, and journal prompts in the chapters to follow will help guide you to your own place of healing. Peace to you...

Stage One: Emotional Shock and Denial

The bottom line is that death and immortality is a harsh reality to grasp and accept. The loss of a beloved companion animal can feel unreal, like a disturbing dream you just can't seem to wake up from. You may have been experiencing anticipatory grief for a long time, your companion animal may have been ill or in the process of dying, yet the finality of death always feels sudden, shocking, and unbelievable. In the days, weeks, or months following a significant loss, it is common to experience shock and denial: a sort of emotional anesthesia. Just as our bodies can experience physical shock in response to pain, so can our psyche experience psychological shock in the wake of emotional trauma such as the death of a cherished companion animal. This is a common coping mechanism that helps us deal with emotions and the shocking reality that is overwhelming and too difficult to process early on. During this initial stage, it is common to experience things such as; emotional numbness, feeling emotionally "frozen," denial, or repression of painful emotions. During this stage, it is also common to experience dissociative symptoms such as; derealization, depersonalization, observing what is going on from afar, or being in an emotional/ cognitive fog or dream-like state. Many grieving pet owners also find themselves searching and calling out for their beloved companion animal in an effort to reaffirm the reality that they are gone and break through the shock and denial. The experience of shock and denial is commonly mistaken for lack of caring or feeling. Still, it is important to understand that emotional numbness is a protective response to the trauma that will lessen over time. It is very common to go in and out of this stage and for it to be triggered by painful circumstances such as; picking up or viewing the ashes, finding pieces of fur or an unexpected toy, looking at old pictures or videos, or running into a friend who may not know your loved one has died, etc.

While there are things you can actively do to support yourself through this stage, you should not attempt to push the natural course of grieving early on. It can be counterproductive to force yourself out of shock and denial too soon since doing so may reinforce the natural defenses already in place. The grieving process is very delicate and needs to be respected and honored in a way that allows for an organic unfolding towards your healing. As we already know, there is no predetermined time frame for the grieving process; however, when the time is right, you will eventually begin to acknowledge the reality of your loss. Depending on circumstances, it could take a few weeks to a few months before the reality of the loss begins to sink in. Your grieving process starts when you move from a place of shock and denial to one of acknowledging the permanency and reality of the death. Even though it feels unusual, shock is part of the process of dealing with painful and traumatic experiences, and in time, it will lessen.

Below are some suggestions to help gently ease and guide your way through shock and denial:

- **Find "safe" friends that understand your pain and that you are comfortable talking to about the loss.** Since you may not be feeling or are feeling numb, you may not talk about your feelings at this very early stage, but talking about the *death and circumstances* surrounding your loss can be helpful.

- **You may need to repeat the details of the death over and over.** This is healthy and natural as it helps to concretize the trauma and bring a sense of reality to the loss. Recite and recount what has been lost as often as you need.

- **Don't pretend things are okay when things certainly are not!** Be honest with yourself and others regarding what you are feeling or not feeling. It is better to talk about it than keep it in; pretending everything is okay does not make everything okay and, in the end, will only make your grief much more difficult to work through.

- **Eventually, you will be ready to face the reality of "death" squarely in the face by calling it what it is.** Challenge yourself to say it, name it, spell it, etc.

- **Gently and slowly confront reminders as opposed to avoiding them.** This includes things like people and situations that you associate with your deceased companion animal, look at old photos and videos, visit the grave, view the ashes, visit special places you have gone to together, touch toys, blankets, and other belongings.

- **Create and surround yourself with "linking objects" during this stage.** These are items of your deceased companion animal that helps remind you of your special bond and aids you in feeling connected and close to them. Having these linking objects close by can help provide a sense of comfort that can lend itself to gently merging out of the shock and denial stage.

Reflective Journal Prompts for Shock and Denial

Following, you will find reflective questions designed to help you process through and gain insight into the Shock and Denial stage of your grieving process.

When I think of the days and week right after you passed, some of the things I experienced were:

- disbelief
- repression of painful feelings
- dissociation
- emotional numbness
- feelings of derealization
- feelings of depersonalization
- feeling as if I were in a dream
- calling out and searching for you

How I felt (or didn't feel) in the days and weeks after you died:

_____

_____

_____

_____

_____

_____

_____

_____

_____

Friends or family members that were most supportive following your death and how they helped me:

_____

_____

_____

_____

_____

_____

_____

_____

_____

The people, places, and situations that I associate with you and places I avoid are:

_____

_____

_____

_____

_____

_____

_____

_____

The first time I viewed your ashes or visited your grave and how it felt for me:

_____

_____

_____

_____

_____

_____

_____

_____

_____

_____

Some of the things I did in the days and weeks following your death that helped to make me feel close to you:

_____

_____

_____

_____

_____

_____

_____

Some of the things I did in the days and weeks following your death that served to help me forget:

_____

_____

_____

_____

_____

_____

_____

_____

_____

_____

Some of the things I did to help comfort and take care of myself in the days and weeks after you passed:

_____

_____

_____

_____

_____

_____

_____

In the days and weeks after you passed, I found myself calling out and searching for you even though I knew you were gone. Some of my calling and searching out behaviors and the purpose they served were:

_____

_____

_____

_____

_____

_____

_____

_____

_____

As I work towards being able to acknowledge the reality of your death, I feel:

_____

_____

_____

_____

_____

_____

_____

_____

_____

_____

_____

_____

_____

_____

_____

_____

My *Reflections on Shock and Disbelief*:

Real Life Vignettes of Companion Animal Loss and Shock and Disbelief

The following are real-life narratives taken from clinical, research, and book interviews that highlight the stages of Shock and Disbelief. These are just a few examples of how grieving pet owners describe their experience of acceptance and reconciliation, and perhaps you might find validation, hope, and connection through these brief vignettes.

Cindy C. and Canine Companion Tenor:

The day Tenor died is something I will never forget, and even eight months later, I can remember what it felt like for me. That moment I found out, the day after, the week after, and even months after. It was as if I could not accept the reality of what had happened. I knew in my mind that she was gone, but I would do odd things like calling out for her and look for her. It all just happened so fast that I could not go from one day having her here with me to the next, without warning, her being gone. I would go outside and scream her name and call her to come into the house. I would ask my husband where she was. Like I knew she was gone, but I just could not believe it. How could that have happened so fast, you know? If I called her and she did not come, then I had to accept that she was indeed gone. But I was still in such a state of shock. I would go in and out of these phases of calling out for her and searching for her to not feeling anything, just nothingness. It was like I could only handle it in manageable doses. I now know that my reaction was to me from the painful feelings that were underneath and part of being in emotional shock and denial.

Rachel and Canine Companion Charley:

I was told that Charley got through the surgery fine and to come in the next morning to pick her up. I even visited with her the afternoon of the surgery and she seemed fine. When I got there the next morning, they brought me back to a room and I sat there for what seemed like a very long time before the Vet came in. That is when I knew something was wrong. When he told me the news that Charley died in the middle of the night, I just remember demanding to see her. I began searching the facility for her. Even when they showed me her body, I still thought they were playing a trick on me in the back of my mind that it was not really her body. After that, I remember for the next two months just feeling as if I were floating, like my feet were not touching the ground, and I was watching my life from a distance and not really there; a guess feeling detached from everything and all feelings. People would tell me I was doing "well," but the fact was that I was not doing "well" at all. It was all too much for me. I would call out for her to come get her dinner every night. I would just call her name and wait for her to come. I would keep calling out for her. I would call down for her at the top of the steps. I would call her name thinking that it was all a big joke and she would magically appear. I could not accept that she was gone. That was such a confusing time for me, and of course, I had minimal support from friends and family, as they did not understand. Eventually, the shock did pass.

Carolyn C. and Canine Companion Nikki:

Once the decision was made to euthanize Nikki, I went into an odd "let's get business done" mode. Almost like, let's just do this, and we can all go home together. I just shut off from my emotions so that I could follow through with the procedure. I held her as she was given the injection and whispered in her ear, and stroked her beautiful fur. I held her so close to me that I could feel her beating heart, and then I could feel it stop just seconds after the injection. After that, I just went numb and really did not remember much of the weeks that followed. I just remember a lot of crying, feeling numb and detached, like I was in a dream. I remember walking around as if I were half alive, like I was in a coma. I would go from not feeling my body, let alone my emotions, to screaming out for Nikki. It was as if I would be in shut down mode for a while, and then I would turn on and freak out by actually going out to our back yard and call for her. I would yell for her to come to me over and over again. I would go out to our special parks looking for her. I don't know what that was about for me, but that lasted a couple of weeks. I mean, I knew she passed, but I just could not accept it. Maybe that is why I did those things. It feels good to talk about this and share because, but those few weeks and even months I was in a very odd unfamiliar place in terms of my emotions.

Meghan A. and Canine Companion Kay:

Right after I saw Kay being hit by a car, I let out a primitive scream, and I ran to her knowing right away that she was dead. I remember feeling a surge of lightning go through me and then nothing. My husband tells me I was just walking around in my policewoman mode even though I was not on duty. I do not remember, though. The next day and the next couple of months, I went on with business as usual, but looking back, I was not feeling anything at all, not even sadness, and this is odd. It was as if I just shut down. But I did find myself searching for some sort of proof that maybe she was not dead. I would call out her name a lot, I found myself calling out to her during certain times, I found myself almost looking for her, and then I would jump right back into the not feeling anything at all mode. There were times where I could not feel anything at all and the tears would not come but eventually, they did; like a dam opened, and they flowed continually for a long time. Looking back, I was in shock and denial for a few months. It was not till a few months after Kay died that the tears came, almost like at first, I could not handle the pain. I kept it undercover and I hoped that it was all a big mistake. I knew, in reality, she was gone but I could not accept it. I still struggle, but at least I can feel again and process the loss.

"*There is a sacredness in tears. They are not the mark of weakness, but of power. They speak more eloquently than ten thousand tongues. They are the messengers of overwhelming grief, of deep contrition, and of unspeakable love.*"
-Washington Irving

Stage Two: Painful Emotions

As touched on in the previous chapter, you may find yourself in a state of shock and denial as a way to defend against the painful emotions that naturally occur immediately following the death of your companion animal. Once the shock and denial begin to fade, it is common to feel a strong surge of painful emotions as you begin to understand and acknowledge the permanency of the death. Though you may vacillate between shock and painful emotions, you will find yourself *feeling* the pain and sadness much more than before. The emotional pain you feel is a normal and expected reaction to losing your beloved companion animal. This is worth repeating because many people in your life may unintentionally cause you to feel that your loss is not important or worthy of grieving. *The intense emotional pain you feel is a normal and expected reaction to the death of your companion animal.* The grieving process does not discriminate, and it is important not to judge your emotions but instead acknowledge them and allow your feelings to find healthy forms of expression. During this stage, you may find yourself blocking out times when your grief hits front and center, but pushing away or suppressing your grief does not bypass it; it is still there, waiting to be expressed and tended to. It is far better to tune into those moments when grief hits you and reminds yourself to pause, reflect, and be mindful of what you feel. By paying attention to those moments of deep sadness and grief, you will begin to understand what you need at that moment and, going forward, to heal, manage, and reconcile your feelings. The heartbreaking emotions of your grief will ebb and flow, sometimes randomly, sometimes predictably, and may at times seem to take on a life of their own.

Some of the emotions that you may experience after the death of your companion animal are: anger, depression, sadness, guilt, fear, anxiety, lowered self-esteem, helplessness, irritability, somatic complaints and grief pangs. Grief pangs are waves of sudden, un-predictable, and very intense feelings of emotional distress. While grief pangs can feel overwhelming, they are part of the normal grieving process, especially in the first few months after a significant loss. While grief pangs may seem to come out of nowhere, many times they are precipitated by a trigger or event that reminds you of your companion animal such as; finding a piece of your pet's fur, seeing or touching your pet's toys or other belongings, finding an old photograph, waking up and finding your pet is not beside you, meeting someone you haven't seen for a while who asks about your pet, going to places that you associate with your pet, and/or a special song or scent that reminds you of your pet. Grief (both normal and complicated) will often present in a similar pattern as clinical depression and can last months and, in some cases, longer. So, how can we tell if what we are experiencing is grief or clinical depression? Many grieving people worry if they are grieving "correctly" or if what they are feeling is "normal." It is important to understand the difference between clinical depression and the intense sadness that accompanies grief. Grief is the reaction to a loss, but not just an emotional reaction to the loss of our loved one; it also affects us spiritually, physically, cognitively, and socially. We all grieve differently based on our personality, previous losses, relationship with our loved one, spiritual beliefs, and cultural influence. The deep sadness you feel after losing your companion animal serves a specific purpose. When you have moments of deep sorrow, you naturally turn inward, and you slow down and become enveloped in a protective cocoon that causes you to lose some of your focus on the outside world; this is part of the healing process. While grieving, you will have bad days and painful moments, but eventually, in time, how you feel will change and how you engage with your grief changes. You slowly learn to adjust and adapt to your loss, and it becomes more manageable over time. Clinical depression, on the other hand, is not intermittent; it is persistent, ongoing, never changing, and typically has no external or environmental cause. While the deep sadness associated with grief is usually more focused on feelings surrounding our loss, clinical depression often has a negative self-focus, which can become distorted with feelings of worthlessness, guilt, and despair. If your symptoms are not going away or if you have a history of depression, it is important to reach out to a mental health professional for support and treatment. Some of the painful emotions of grief that share a similar pattern with clinical depression are:

- constant, pervasive, and severe sadness, anxiety, or feelings of emptiness

- feelings of guilt, helplessness, and/or hopelessness

- loss of interest in hobbies and normal daily activities

- physical aches that don't go away with treatment and have no physical cause

- suicidal thoughts or suicide attempts

- changes in appetite

- sleep disturbances and change in sleep patterns

It is common to experience physical symptoms as a normal part of your grieving process. Although physical symptoms may be primary to your grief, it is important to consult with your physician to rule out a major medical condition for your symptoms. Some of the somatic expressions of grief may include:

- hollow sensation in the stomach

- nausea

- tightness in chest or throat and breathlessness

- muscle weakness

- lightheadedness or dizziness

- fatigue

- weight change
- heart palpitations
- sighing
- headaches
- restlessness
- chills and/or sweats

Because of the profound impact that the loss of a companion animal can have on us, it is common for some people to experience a worsening of preexisting mental health conditions such as; addictive behaviors, PTSD, clinical depression, generalized anxiety / mood disorders, and unresolved grief from prior losses. If the severity of your emotional or physical symptoms are extreme and pervasive at any time, it would be helpful to seek the help of a trained and licensed mental health professional or medical doctor.

During this stage of your grieving process, it is common to wonder if you could have done something different to change the outcome. You may find yourself thinking about the "would have," "should have," "could have" scenarios. Not only is it human nature to second guess ourselves, but it is also a coping skill that helps us to navigate through the difficult terrain of grief. People have a tendency to sort through the ashes of tragedy in search of explanations and meaning, including the death of our companion, especially in traumatic and unexpected situations. Our search for understanding in the seemingly senseless is one of our most instinctual coping skills we can use in the face of hardships like grief. The concept of a life-ending creates a dissonance so harsh that one simply cannot allow it to linger; so, you search, and you sift, and you try to piece the broken things back together again, desperate for it all to make sense. It's common to ask questions after our companion animals die because we want and need answers. You may begin to ask yourself things such as: "why did this happen?" "how could this have happened?" "could I have seen this coming?". When we begin asking ourselves these questions, it is helpful to examine and challenge your narrative, re-examine the reality and reality test as many times as you need until you can come to peace around your decision and outcome. Over time, and as a result of you actively being in your grieving process as opposed to side-stepping it, the intense and painful emotions will become less frequent and less intense. Following are some suggestions and to help you work through the painful emotions of losing your beloved companion animal:

- **Allow yourself to feel the painful emotions of your loss:** As difficult as it can be, the pain of grief is a natural and healthy reaction to the loss of our beloved companion animal. As touched on earlier, grieving pet owners may feel guilty and not entitled to grieve, but keeping your feelings in or hiding them behind a false façade is unhealthy and can lead to maladaptive coping strategies and behaviors. It is commonplace to assume we should "get over" our loss and "move on," but this view is not a realistic way to think about our grief. It is essential to allow yourself the time and space to grieve and feel grief, sadness, anger, depression, despondence, loneliness, etc. Do not minimize your situation or judge yourself for having these feelings. Allow yourself to react in ways authentic to you and help you process and release powerful emotions (even if that means screaming in your car with all the windows up, crying in the shower, or punching a pillow!). It may be necessary to set aside quiet time every day to reflect on your beloved companion animal and give yourself permission to experience any emotions that come up without judgment.

- **Talk with Others:** Choose a few friends or family members who understand what you are going through and be transparent with them about your feelings. Sharing what you are going through with others will help you concretize, process, and release your feelings. Let your friends and family know it is important for you to share your feelings with them and that you are not looking for them to "fix" things but just need them to listen. Verbally reliving the experience is a useful technique to come to terms with the reality of the loss and your emotions, especially when euthanasia is involved. You may find you need to tell and retell your story over and over again. This is normal and to be expected.

- **Find ways to Memorialize your Companion Animal:** Just as we pay tribute to and commemorate our human loved ones who have passed, memorializing our companion animals is helpful to our healing process and provides an outlet for us to cope with difficult and painful emotions. For a comprehensive discussion and ideas on memorializing, please see Chapter Three.

- **Find Creative Outlets for Active Grieving**: There will be times when you just don't feel like talking to others and will feel the need to go inward. Sometimes it can be challenging to find words for what we are going through, and as a result, our emotions can stay inside of us with no way to express them. It is helpful to be "active" with your feelings during these times because the act of creating following a death can be especially cathartic. Consider expressing your feelings through creative activities such as: music, art, dance, writing, photography, cooking, painting, etc. Writing your thoughts and feelings in a journal can be useful as it provides a safe and private outlet for your feelings and provides a link to your beloved pet.

- **Engage in Physical Activity:** Find a physical activity such as swimming, walking, hiking, running, or riding a bicycle to help you cope with your feelings. Exercise and activities like hitting a punching bag or hitting golf balls at a driving range may release frustration or anger. Exercise releases powerful chemicals in our brains, such as endorphins, serotonin, and BDNF (Brain-Derived Neurotropic Factor). These chemicals can help cope with grief because they decrease the stress response, decrease depressive symptoms, and enhance mood.

- **Give Yourself a Respite from Grieving with Mindfulness. We all need a break!** Just as it may be important to set time aside every day to tend to your grieving process, it can also be necessary to take time away from your grieving process. Whether it is a bath, shower, cooking a meal, or a trip to the store, practice mindfulness of being fully "in" the activity. Force yourself to focus on the here and now of what you are doing, even if it is just focusing on your breathing! Sometimes we forget to breathe when we are stressed or grieving. Focusing your attention on something other than your grief is a healthy way to take a momentary break from your grief. Consider practicing daily meditation to calm the mind, relax the body, and instill a sense of inner peace.

- **Keep a routine:** Cultivating a basic routine of everyday activities serves to structure your time and keeps you connected to familiar people and places. This also helps you cultivate a sense of normalcy during a time when things are anything but normal for you. Maintaining a routine can help you stay grounded and centered during a time when your life is anything but.

- **Be patient and allow your grief to unfold at a pace natural for you.** Try not to judge or criticize yourself for not coping as well or healing as quickly as you think you "should." Everyone needs to grieve in a manner and pace that is right for him or her. Be gentle and patient with yourself during this challenging time and have faith in your healing process no matter how slow it may seem. Grief does not necessarily have a "finish" line and is certainly not a sprint to the finish, so be patient with yourself and your individual process.

- **Consider professional counseling or join an in-person or online pet loss support group:** **Seeking counseling by a licensed mental health professional specializing in pet bereavement can help those who are having an extremely difficult** time coping or experiencing complicated grief or clinical depression. Both in-person and on-line pet loss support groups can provide the opportunity to speak with others who are going through similar struggles. Group members can provide encouragement, comfort, guidance, and understanding and help normalize your experience and reassure you that you are not alone in your grief. Some may find the collective grief in a group setting overwhelming, so be sure to limit the amount of time you spend in groups.

Reflective Journal Prompts for Painful Emotions

Following, you will find reflective questions designed to help you process through and gain insight into the Painful Emotions stage of your grieving process.

As my shock and disbelief begin to dissipate, some of the emotions I feel are:

_____

_____

_____

_____

_____

_____

The emotions that are the most predominate and difficult for me are and why:

_____

_____

_____

_____

_____

_____

Some of the ways I express these difficult emotions are:

Some healthy coping techniques I engage in to help process my painful emotions are:

Some of the not so healthy coping techniques I engage in to help process my painful emotions are:

_____

_____

_____

_____

_____

_____

At times, I find myself trying to hide my true feelings from myself and others. The reason I do this and how this makes me feel:

_____

_____

_____

_____

_____

_____

_____

I sometimes find myself engaging in "if only" and "what if" counter-factual thinking. If I were to re-frame these thoughts into a more balanced view, it would look something like this:

_____

_____

_____

_____

_____

_____

_____

As my painful emotions begin to subside or shift, I feel (relief, guilt, remorse, etc.):

_____

_____

_____

_____

_____

_____

_____

My Reflections on Painful Emotions:

Real Life Vignettes of Companion Animal Loss and Painful Emotions

Following are real-life narratives taken from clinical, research, and book interviews that highlight the stage of Painful Emotions discussed in this chapter. These are just a few examples of how grieving pet owners describe their experience of acceptance and reconciliation, and perhaps you might find validation, hope, and connection through these brief vignettes.

Janet K. and Canine Companion Cassie:

After Cassie died, I felt an intensity of agonizing emotions that I have never felt before. I had emotions that were all tangled together, tangled together in a way that I could not figure out where one feeling began, and one ended. I had a lot of anger early on and then depression and extreme sadness. Then as time went on, I began to feel panic and helplessness as if I was lost in a big ocean with no life preserver. I felt so cut off from society because most people did not understand. I remember one evening, in particular, being so angry that Cassie got cancer. My young, healthy Cassie got cancer without warning. Why her? Why now? I use to scream at God for taking the one thing that meant the world to me away from me. Then the flip side would be depression and sadness, and then panic and helplessness began to kick in. It has been close to a year now, and those difficult emotions have calmed down, but sometimes they still come up. I have experienced human loss before and have been able to process that easier. With Cassie, it is just more complicated and different. I still feel as if I will never be quite the same again.

Clair W. and Canine Companion Penny:

The death of Penny was harder than anything I have ever gone through in my life. There was no real predictable pattern to my grieving; I just felt mostly sad and depressed. I was depressed to the point where I could not or did not want to get out of bed in the morning because the reminders were just too painful. The reminders that she was really gone forever. So, the depression just kind of kept me alone and drained me. I had never felt depression before, but I think that is what it was. Yes, I missed her, but my depression almost felt like a heavyweight on my shoulders that only Penny could take away. I also felt very alone. Being without her, I was alone for the first time in many years. Even though I am a grown woman, she kept me safe, so I was jolted into a strange new world that I wanted no part of when she died. I was depressed for close to 3 months. I still feel quite lonely but am able to venture out now. I can still remember that feeling of depression. I have never felt anything like that before in my life, and sometimes it does come up again but not as strong.

Sam K. and Canine Companion Bentley:

It was just so devastating because of how close we were. I remember feeling so many different emotions all at once, but the thing that stands out for me is the anger I had towards the Veterinarian and myself for not being more proactive for my Bentley. The anger tore me apart, and then when I was exhausted from the anger, I would sink into profound sadness. Maybe that is not the right word for it, but I do not know how else to describe it. A sadness that felt so dark and heavy inside of me. I remember becoming so angry because there was no book on this, no road map. So, I read a book on grief of losing a human, and it just did not fit my experience in terms of you feel this then you feel that. I mean, I did experience very similar things, but it made me feel as if something was wrong with me because my experience was very erratic and did fall into some nice neat little package. I just know that I went back and forth between anger and profound sadness. I am feeling better, I mean,

I can talk about it now without breaking down, but the anger and sadness are still there.

Jill L. and Canine Companion Erin:

The deep longing and sadness just blew me away. I actually hurt on a visceral level in my heart, like I had a broken heart, literally. I was just so depressed and sad and had this longing to hold her and pet her one last time. I felt some guilt over not being with her in her final moments and guilt over not really rallying for her. A lot of guilt that I use to beat myself up with. The other thing is I would be walking around like everything was fine, and then out of nowhere, I would be crying and hurting all over again. Without warning this would happen. Sometimes I did not know when or where this would happen. I could be at a restaurant and it would come over me. It felt so out of control and had a lot of anxiety about when and where it would happen. I did not have anyone to talk to about my feelings. The best I got from my friends and family was that I should get another one. Another one? Believe me, if I could get another Erin I would. When people lose spouses or children do we say, "oh, just go get another one"? I think that made it worse for me. The grief still comes and goes but not as severe as it once was. Losing Erin is by far the most painful thing I have ever experienced. It was like going into a black hole. I experienced each sunrise as an insult to Erin's memory, and I would keep the blinds down. I did not want to see the sunlight or the sunset or anything that reminded me of him because it just tore the scab right off. I remember feeling so isolated in my pain, which made the depression and loneliness even worse. It was just a terribly dark time in my life that lasted over six months. I am better now but never the same.

"*Life is eternal, and love is immortal, and death is only a horizon; and a horizon is nothing save the limit of our sight.*"
- Rossiter Worthington Raymond

Stage Three: Living in the Past

When someone irreplaceable, such as our companion animal, is gone, it's very hard not to look back and grieve for what life was like in the past. It isn't easy to accept that certain moments, feelings, and realities from our yesteryear may always feel surreal and just out of our reach. It makes complete sense that we would want to hold on, if not, white knuckle, the time in our lives when our beloved companion animals were alive and well. This concept lends itself to one of the stages of grief associated with the death of a companion animal that is distinct from what we typically see in human loss and is referred to as "Living in the Past." Grieving pet owners who experience this stage of grief may feel emotionally and physically "stuck" in the past. In both my clinical work and research experience, grieving pet owners describe this stage of grief as; a sense of ambivalence towards the future, resistance to change, lack of desire to engage in new activities, and a desire to engage in the same activities and patterns as when the pet was still alive. During this stage, it can be challenging to re-engage in life once again. It is common to focus on a time when your beloved companion animal was alive and well; you may feel guilty doing things without your pet and have the desire to withdraw from people and activities.

Living in the Past is seen more frequently in companion animal loss than in human loss, but why is this? One reason is the disenfranchised nature and lack of emotional and social support make it very difficult to work through and resolve grief associated with the loss of a companion animal. Living (or being "stuck") in the past is an outcome of unresolved and painful feelings, and the connection to your companion animal is preserved through engagement in familiar emotions, daily patterns, and activities. In this sense, the experience of Living in the Past serves to link you to your companion animal, and the concept of "moving on" is not surprisingly met with resistant. This resistance is normal and expected until such time that you have adjusted to and reconciled your loss. The task of mourning our companion animals while still being present to our lives in the moment is one of the most difficult tasks of grieving. While still struggling with your loss, you may also feel the need to carry on with "normal" daily activities. This polarization of emotions can be the source of additional tension and conflict, and it is normal to feel a sense of ambivalence from experiencing these conflicting emotions at the same time; i.e., the desire to continue on and re-engage in your life vs. the desire to stay in the past when your beloved was alive and well. If you find you are struggling with being present in the here and now because it is just too painful, remind yourself that you can keep loving someone long after they die; death ends a life, not a relationship. You may not be able to hold them or cuddle with them, but you can still love them every bit as much as you work towards opening to life in the present moment. Commit yourself and your companion animal to take positive steps to heal and live the best life you can; do this in memory and tribute to them. Following are tips to help you move from Living in the Past to living more fully in the present:

- **Give Yourself Permission to Mourn the Past While Living in the Present and Construct a New Sense of Self.** It's heartbreaking to realize the days of sharing your life with your companion animal are gone, most certainly a deep and unspeakable sadness. It is common to alternate between the "you" grieving your past and feeling like you are losing parts of yourself and your old life little by little, and the "you" engaging in your current life, growing, changing and evolving. While straddling these two opposing worlds, it is possible to merge your past AND your present to construct a new sense of self and purpose. Although these two 'selves' may seem to be in direct contradiction to each another, realize that you have the ability to be both at the same time and that you are a work in progress, always evolving. Remind yourself that it is possible and healthy to mourn your past while still being grateful for and engaged in the present.

- **Accept that guilt can be a consequence of re-engaging in life again and can pressure you to stay in the past.** Guilt is one of the most powerful and crippling of all human emotions; it is the greatest destroyer of our emotional energy. Whenever you feel 'guilty' about doing things in the present without your companion animal, replace your guilt with a memory of happy times and cherished moments of your beloved. Carry the love you have for your beloved companion animal WITH you as you continue on in your life.

- **Remind yourself that even though your relationship has changed, it is still a relationship;** It is okay and healthy to have an ongoing connection with your companion animal. Yes, the relationship has changed, but it is nevertheless still a relationship; remember, death ends a life, not a relationship. Allow the emotional presence embodied within you to continue to inform your life in positive ways. Doing this can help lessen the pain of grief and maintain your connection. Love is stronger than death and stronger than grief; allow the love you continue to have to inform your life as you work towards re-engaging and adjusting to life without your companion animal.

- **Make a list of all the qualities you most admire about your companion animal.** From that list, envision ways that YOU can continue to bring those attributes and qualities forth into the world. In doing so, you create a "living memory" of your companion animal, and they will continue to live on through your actions and intentions. Remember, "moving on" is not about "leaving behind" or "letting go";

it's about continuing to honor your relationship in a way that recognizes all your beloved brought to your life and the world. What better way to do that than become the things you most admire about them!

- **Chose a few momentous "linking objects" to carry with you.** Linking Objects are items that "link" us to our deceased loved one. They are items that belonged to our deceased companion animal and remind us of positive experiences and feelings and help to comfort and give us peace. They are powerful and symbolic items that help you stay connected to them as you begin re-engaging and adjusting to life without their physical presence by your side.

- **Find a meaningful way to commemorate the death of your beloved and memorialize his or her life.** While culturally embedded, memorializing is something most of us do after the loss of a human loved one without thought or question. It is an essential component of our grieving process because it allows us to pay tribute to and honor our cherished companion animals. Memorials and ceremony also serve to draw the death into the present moment and encourages you to be more present to the here and now, which can help if you are having difficulty re-engaging in life or feeling stuck in the past. See Chapter Three for ideas and suggestions on memorializing your companion animal.

My daily patterns that remain the same since you died:

_____

_____

_____

_____

_____

_____

_____

My daily patterns that have changed since you died and how this feels for me:

_____

_____

_____

_____

_____

_____

_____

_____

_____

When I go to places that were special to us, it makes me feel:

As time passes on, some of the ways that I resist change are:

As time passes on, some ways that I embrace change are:

Finding a balance between my life when you were alive and my life without you here can best be described as:

The idea of relinquishing some of the past and integrating new roles into my life brings about feelings of:

_____

_____

_____

_____

_____

_____

Life without you here is like:

_____

_____

_____

_____

_____

_____

_____

_____

As opposed to undoing the tie that binds me to you, some ways that your continued presence informs my life is:

_____

_____

_____

_____

_____

_____

_____

Finding a balance between my life when you were alive and my life without you here can be best described as:

_____

_____

_____

_____

_____

_____

_____

_____

Even though our relationship has changed, it is still a relationship, and this is how I can continue to bring you forward with me in my life:

My Reflections on Living in the Past:

Real Life Vignettes of Companion Animal Loss and Living in the Past

Following are real-life narratives taken from clinical, research, and book interviews that highlight the stage of Living in the Past discussed in this chapter. These are just a few examples of how grieving pet owners describe their experience of acceptance and reconciliation, and perhaps you might find validation, hope, and connection through these brief vignettes.

Cindy F. and Canine Companion Tenor:

As I look back, I seemed to have been stuck in my past life when Tenor was alive. I had no interest in 'moving on' as so many people told me I was supposed to do. I maintained the same patterns everyday as if Tenor was still with me and refused to change my routine. I seemed to have been trapped in the past because I couldn't bear to do things without her, so I wouldn't do anything new, only things we did together. At first, it was okay because I needed to do that to keep her close, but after a while it lost its purpose. People were beginning to say things to me, and of course, it would just anger me back then. I missed her so very much and could not bear to leave the past behind, so I would do all kinds of things to stay focused on what life was like when she was alive. Moving into the future without her seemed like an insult to her memory, and I just could not do it. I think that on some level it reinforced that she was gone, and I still could not accept that even after four or five months after she died. It is still difficult for me now, but I am a bit better and have even added some new things to my life. I still get sad when I think about how she would have loved these things, but I do not feel guilty anymore. I guess it is just the natural course of time.

Christine V. and Canine Companion Sunny:

Staying in my old pattern of doing things was the only thing that kept me connected to Sunny, and people around me tried to take that away from me. I needed to stay in the same patterns and same routines as when she was alive; I did not want to go to new places or meet new people or change anything from our life together. People did not understand that I needed to stay close to all of her things and maintain my previous way of being because that was the only thing I had left of her. Beginning a new life in a world without her was not tolerable, so I stayed in the past where I found comfort in the memories of Sunny and me. Eventually, I realized that I needed to re-engage in life and eventually found a way back, but it was and, at times, is still comforting to repeat those old patterns. I still find comfort in those things, but the difference now, years later, is that it does not stop me from living in the present. I bring her with me everywhere I go; she is in my heart and a part of my soul.

Roger and Canine Companion Murphy:

It has not really been that long since my Murphy died, but it feels like an eternity, and everyone is telling me that I need to 'move on,' but I don't know what 'moving on' means. He was a part of my life for 15 years and those 15 years were wrapped around his every move, his every need as I do not have human children. I would take him almost everywhere with me, including work; he would hike and run with me and be my companion on out of state trips visiting family. My entire life routine was about Murphy and me. Perhaps in retrospect, that was not a good thing, but at the time, it seemed like a perfect thing. After he died, the only way to make it through my day was to continue to do everything the EXACT the same way as when he was alive. My daily routine and schedule stayed identical because that was the only way I felt close to him; changing my life in any way brought about such painful grief pangs that I just stayed with my feet very much planted in the 'past.' I think for a period of time it helped me to cope, but after a while, I knew I needed to be present to the life in front of me; not behind me. Through time and therapy, I learned ways to bring Murphy along with me and was assured that in doing so, I was not leaving him behind. He is still with me every single day.

Nick C. and Canine Companion Maddy:

What stands out the most for me is how difficult it was to go out of the house after Maddie passed over. I just could not bear to be away from the house after she died; even two or three months after she died, it was still difficult. I wanted everything to stay the same and did everything in my power to make sure that would happen. This may sound weird, but I would pour her food every morning and evening at her regular feeding time. I was doing this not just a few days or weeks after, but months after. I would do things as if she were still alive; I felt so isolated and alone because I was not going out and doing anything outside of work. After work, I would rush home as usual, even though I did not have to anymore. I remember one time I decided to go for a swim after work, and after a few minutes, I broke down and felt so bad that I was doing something I enjoyed, and she was dead. I got out of the pool and just went home; I could not bear to be doing things without her. Friends would say to me, 'it is time to move on,' and I would just refuse to do this 'moving on' thing. I wanted just to be where she was or at least where the memories of her were. It has gotten better after a year, but I still am not fond of this idea of moving on. Moving on to leave her behind? I would rather not, but I now know that I bring her with me every breath of every day; she is with me as long as I am alive; she remains alive in spirit. It has taken a good year to get to that point.

Janet T. and Canine Companion Cassie:

There were so many things that were hard for me. Too many to mention, but if I were to choose one, I think it would be the pressure I felt to re-enter into the land of the living, back to life again. I felt as if I would be leaving Cassie behind if I were to move on, so I chose not to move on with my life. I spent so much of my time thinking about the time in my life when Cassie was still alive. I felt so guilty about doing things without her, so I would just stay home and not do anything. I just wanted it to be the way it was when Cassie was alive. I really had no interest in doing things that did not include her. I was not depressed; I just felt so bad that she was not here with me anymore, so I just shut the door- literally- shut everyone out of my life. At that time in my grieving process, I felt that it would be a dishonor to Cassie to do things without her. I just wanted to be home around her things and look at her pictures and videos day after day after day, even months after she passed. When I did try to go out and do new things, I would be bombarded with this horrible guilt, like you know, "how could I enjoy life without her"? I really wanted my old life back, which was one of the biggest struggles for me. I am better now, but I still get sad at times and still feel some guilt about continuing on with life. I fear that I may lose contact with her the more that time goes by, but I am learning that I carry her with me through memory and keep her safely tucked away in my heart where she will forever be; death does not change that.

"There is a land of the living and a land of the
dead, and the bridge is love, the only survival,
the only meaning."
-Thornton Wilder, The Bridge
of San Luis Rey

Stage Four: Acceptance and Reconciliation

Grief is like a gentle echo that is always in the background and sometimes makes a front and center appearance. Nevertheless, if you are like most people, you will eventually come to a place of Acceptance and Reconciliation. Intellectually, you know you really don't recover from your grief in the sense that everything is restored back to the way it was before the loss of your companion animal. You know that life will never be quite the same, and in the beginning of your grieving process, it is so very difficult to accept the finality of your loss and all that it means to your life. You are in the very beginning stages of a process of "reconciliation" where you learn, over time, to adjust and adapt to a new and different way of living. The stage of Acceptance and Reconciliation is unique for each person but generally speaking, Acceptance and Reconciliation is the process of accepting, adapting, adjusting, and re-engaging in your life after the death of a loved one. While you will always miss your beloved companion animal, and there will always be a special place in your heart reserved just for them, this stage of your process is informed by a sense of peace surrounding your loss and openness to accepting a slightly different version of your life and your sense of Self.

Acceptance is the point when you can acknowledge the inevitability and permanency of the death of your companion animal. It's not that you are "over" the loss, but your mind, body, and emotions are finally able to accept what has occurred, and you see it as something you can incorporate into your everyday life, thoughts, and feelings. At this stage, you are better able to make sense of what has happened and frame your experience and emotions in a way that supports re-investing your emotional energy in new ways. The death no longer consumes the entirety of your emotional being, and you become open to engaging in your life once again without guilt or remorse. This occurs slowly as you make efforts to integrate the new reality of how your life will be without your beloved. Remember, Acceptance does not imply you no longer miss your beloved companion animal or that you forget about or are leaving them behind. Acceptance does not mean that you feel good about the loss. Most people never feel okay that their loved one is gone. This stage is about accepting that your new reality cannot be changed and how this new reality will impact your life and relationships moving forward. Acceptance does not mean we ignore the loss and pretend all is fine; it means we can agree to the terms of our new life as we begin taking responsibility and ownership of our life once again. Remember, death ends a life, not a relationship, and all the love you ever had remains forever a part of you; you can continue to nurture that love while at the same time acknowledging that your beloved companion animal is no longer physically by your side.

Reconciliation is the on-going process of adapting and adjusting to an environment and life without your companion animal. There are many secondary and existential losses we experience after the death of a beloved companion animal, and adjusting to a life without them requires you to redefine your day-to-day life and reconstruct the meaning of who you are in the context of your life. For example:

- Your companion animal may have been the source of emotional affection, support, and comfort. We all know each bond is unique and different and cannot simply be "replaced." Because your bond can never be replaced or replicated, you will have to adjust to the norms and expectations of new relationships.

- Your beloved was a member of your family, so their death will cause a change in your family structure. Death, trauma, and transition can impact the entire family unit; we all grieve differently, which can strain the family dynamic, requiring a time of adjustment.

- Grieving pet owners are often shocked when their family and friends are not supportive or understanding and/or begin disappearing. Because of this, you may feel the need to redefine your support system and social circle.

- Especially in the case of caring for a sick or elderly companion animal whereby much of your role was that of a primary caretaker and/or maternal figure, you may need to redefine your role after the loss. Because of your loss, you will have to take on and adjust to new roles resulting in a shift in responsibility, identity, purpose, and priority.

- Your identity and self-perception may be challenged as a result of your loss, and the challenges faced. This may impact how you view yourself; Do you think less of yourself for the things you have struggled with since the loss? Are you proud of the adversity you have successfully overcome? How you see and experience yourself after a loss is ever-changing and ever-evolving, requiring you to adapt and change to the inner and outer landscape of your new life.

Sometimes, unexpectedly or out of nowhere, something big happens: death, illness, transition, or a traumatic event. This can make a person question everything; self, the world, faith, security, significance, meaning, trust, and morality. Fractures in one's fundamental understanding of life can be one of the most difficult adjustments a person will ever have to make. In reconciling a beloved companion animal's death, one often has to redefine their sense of self and belief system, which has a ripple effect on how they relate to pretty much everything. Your feeling of loss will not completely disappear, but it will lessen over time, and your grief will become less frequent and less intense. Eventually, faith for a renewed life will emerge as you are able to make commitments to your future life, realizing that your companion animal will never be forgotten, knowing that your life can and will move forward. Yes, indeed, your life will forever be different as a result of your loss, and you will be a slightly different version of yourself as you grow and evolve around your loss and grief.

However, reconciliation is not just the capacity to adjust and adapt to life without your companion animal by your side; It is the internalization and embodiment of the sacredness they brought to your life. Imagine creative ways to actualize and give expression to the qualities you most admired about your companion animals and all the goodness they brought to your life. In doing so, you construct and give birth to a "living memory" of your companion animal, enabling them to live on through you; through your thoughts, intentions, and actions. Reconciling the pain of losing a cherished companion animal is, in part, about being a reflection of the sacredness they brought to your life and walking in that light every day of your life. By creating something greater than the pain of your suffering, you remind yourself that **the love you have for your cherished companion animal will always be stronger than their death, and your love will always be more powerful than your grief.** In reconciling our loss, we are not forgetting about or leaving our companion animal behind. Instead, we come to a place where we have internalized and embodied the memory of our companion animal, keeping them forever present in our heart and evolving life, allowing us to come to a place of peace surrounding the loss. Become those very things you most admire about your beloved companion animal and pay tribute to them every day. By doing this, we honor their memory and keep their spirits very much alive! As you continue to reconcile your loss, you may find yourself taking three steps ahead and two steps back, but you are continuing to heal and figure out how to "be" in a world without your loved one. Life does continue, never the same, but always and forever enriched by your beloved's presence in your past, current, and future life.

You know you have reached the stage of Acceptance and Reconciliation when you begin to experience some of the following:

- Your earlier painful feelings begin to diminish in their frequency, and intensity.

- You can think of your deceased companion animal with less emotional and psychological suffering.

- You are better able to acknowledge and accept the complete reality of the death.

- You can talk about your companion animal without overwhelming emotions.

- You have a willingness to re-engage in life and form new meaning structures and relationships.

- There is movement from living in the past to living in the present, marked by an investment in your present and future.

- You begin to re-engage in daily living and new activities that did not involve your companion animal.

- There is restored ambivalence and the ability to experience life without your companion animal.

- You have formed a different relation to and with your companion animal; an internalization of the love that is now a part of your subjective emotional world; a "living love."

- You no longer feel guilty experiencing moments of happiness.

- You may consider bringing in a new pet to your household.

- You learn to effectively experience and express the reality of the death in a manageable and healthy way.

- You learn to develop a new self-identity based on a life without your companion animal.

- You learn safe ways to experience and express your grief and how to mourn while still taking care of yourself and your current life.

Reflective Journal Prompts for Acceptance and Reconciliation

Following, you will find reflective questions designed to help you process through and gain insight into the Acceptance and Reconciliation stage of your grieving process.

Some of the ways I continue to keep you present in my evolving life are:

_____

_____

_____

_____

_____

_____

_____

_____

_____

_____

_____

_____

_____

_____

How my life has changed since you died and how I feel about these changes:

_____

_____

_____

_____

_____

_____

_____

Some of the ways I have changed since you died and how I feel about that:

_____

_____

_____

_____

_____

_____

_____

_____

Some of the ways that I continue to keep your memory alive in my life:

_____

_____

_____

_____

_____

_____

_____

Some of the ways that you continue to inform my life and how our relationship continues on, even in your physical absence:

_____

_____

_____

_____

_____

_____

_____

_____

As I walk through my life, I know it is healthy and natural to continue to keep the memory of you alive in my life. Some ways that I do this are:

_____

_____

_____

_____

_____

_____

_____

If you were here right now, this is what I would say to you:

_____

_____

_____

_____

_____

_____

_____

_____

Five words that best describe my experience of having known and loved you:

1.

2.

3.

4.

5.

As I continue to make an effort to re-engage in life without your physical presence, I can internalize and embody the things you symbolized in your life and through your death. I create this living memory of you by:

_____

_____

_____

_____

_____

_____

_____

_____

_____

_____

My Reflections on Acceptance and Reconciliation

Real Life Vignettes of Acceptance and Reconciliation:

Following are real-life narratives taken from clinical, research, and book interviews that highlight the stage of Acceptance and Reconciliation discussed in this chapter. These are just a few examples of how grieving pet owners describe their experience of acceptance and reconciliation, and perhaps you might find validation, hope, and connection through these brief vignettes.

Natashia E. and Canine Companion Samantha:

It has taken close to two years to say for certainty that I have landed in a place of accepting that she is gone and never coming back. I have begun re-engaging in life once again; not necessarily without her but with her being a part of my heart and soul. The sun rose and set around her; my days were wrapped around her and her needs, her special needs, so in that sense, her life defined my life. She was like an extension of me in so many ways that I literally felt like half a person after she died. It seemed like I needed to learn how to walk and breathe again without her. I slowly learned to adjust and adapt to life without her and no longer feel consumed by the grief. Through therapy, I learned how to keep her memory alive by being her voice in this life. I will never stop missing her, and the pain of losing her will always be there, but it is not always front and center. I have learned to carry on and bring her memory forward into the future with me. She will always be a part of me. My message of hope to others is that if I can get to this place of acceptance and reconciliation, then so can you because this was the greatest of all hurts I ever experienced and lived to tell.

Jill C. and Canine Companion Erin:

I think I have come to a place of acceptance that she is gone in physical form, but I can still feel her spirit in me because of the things I do every day that serve to honor her memory. The more the painful feelings fade away, the more I can feel her spirit and internalize our relationship. If I did not have that spiritual connection, I might not feel okay about accepting the realization that she is gone. She is very much still alive in my heart and a part of my soul, and that is something I can accept. I feel like I have come to a more stable place, been through a very dark storm, and have come to the calm that occurs right after the storm. I believe that acknowledging the reality of her death and being okay with it has allowed me to connect with life once again.

Rachel M. and Canine Companion Lucy:

For me, accepting and coming to terms is kind of like getting used to an IV in your arm. Initially, the IV hurts but after a few minutes, you really do not notice it as much; you don't notice how uncomfortable it is. You just get used to the needle being in your arm; that becomes your new reality. It still may be uncomfortable, but you learn to deal with the needle in your arm; you accept it. In terms of Lucy, I am not as depressed, my anxiety has decreased, the nightmares are gone, I'm going out again and trying to do the things I use to do, and I have less guilt over it. I have acknowledged to myself that she is gone, is not coming back, and that I need to carry on with my life. So, in that sense I have come to accept this new reality. That does not mean I like it; I do not want to have an IV jabbed into my arm, but I can accept that it is there and I think that made it easier for me. The same thing with Lucy's loss; accepting that she is gone forever has helped me carry on.

Heather and Feline Companion Misty:

I think now after one year, I have come to accept that this is how my life will be. I think I am okay with it because I know he is still with me here in my heart and is not in pain any longer. Somehow through the past year, I have been able to continue on with my life, not the same as when Misty was still alive, but still recognizing and acknowledging that it is okay to enjoy life once again. It was not as if I woke up one day and said to myself, "wow, I feel better; I am over it." It was a very slow process that, up until now, one year later, I do not even think I realized. I guess what I am saying is that my experience right now is one of acceptance and finding peace as a result of that. I am allowing myself to receive life once again. As a result of that, I can accept the permanency of Misty's death or maybe it is the other way around. That through accepting her death, I can take life in once again.

Sam and Canine Companion Rocky:

I think I have come to a place of acceptance on some level, but an acceptance of a reality that my life will never be as it was. I had people tell me how it will not always be so hard and how I will have acceptance and peace around Rocky death one day. Quite honestly, the peace is not there, and yes, there is an acceptance that she is never coming back, and I am slowly learning that it is not just okay but necessary for me to live my life. I bring her with me as I re-engaged in my life again. I am not at complete peace with it; that will take timea lot of time, but after a year, I am finally coming up for air again.

Transcendence and Continuance: Moving On... Together...

There is something beyond the final stage of grief that embraces the idea of symbolically and emotionally carrying our loved ones with us as we continue on in our lives. Continuance is not so much a stage as it is an emotional experience and psychological stance around how we choose to join with our grieving process and our loved one's memory as we move forward in our lives. Continuance in your grieving process is about bringing the essence of your relationship with you as you continue to walk through the days and years of your life. Continuance is a delicate balance between engaging in a new life without your beloved companion animal by your side while at the same time continuing to honor all the wonderful gifts they brought to your life. While we all go through grief differently, collectively, we have benefited from the idea that some commonalities and patterns help define and structure how we experience the loss of someone we love, which of course includes the loss of a companion animal. As noted in the previous chapters, the stage model of grief provides a wonderful framework for understanding and reflecting on a process that can be one of the most difficult of all human emotions; it provides a guide and structure to our grieving experience. However, the stage model can be misleading because it fails to recognize grief's infinite nature and implies there is an ending to our process. The reality is there is no finish line to our process; the finish line is more an allusive ideal than a tangible goal. Our grief does not have an expiration date, and it will continue to inform and be a part of our evolving self and life. In fact, healing is a continual and ever-evolving process of turning into the you that is still here despite your companion animal's death. Many grieving pet owners feel pressured and/or pathologized by others if they do not put a decisive period at the end of their grieving process. Most of us have been taught to think about the death of a loved one as something we are expected to "get over" in a predetermined amount of time; however, in actuality, this could not be further from the truth. A common cold is something we "get over," not the death of a loved one. Especially in companion animal loss, we are expected to minimize our pain and the length of time we mourn our loss. We are expected to bounce right back to our lives as if nothing significant has changed. Those around us may even try to convince us something is wrong if we don't fit into a predetermined pattern of grieving, and we may begin to question if how we feel is normal. The idea that time heals all is not always true, especially in the case of grief, and the expectation that you are to "let go" and "move on" understandably leads us to feel conflicted. When we speak of "letting go" and "moving on," we visualize turning our back and walking away. But why would we want to walk away from a love, from a relationship that has been the very fabric of our lives? As discussed in the previous chapter, instead of thinking about the death of your companion animal as something you need to "get over," re-frame your thoughts in a way that supports the idea of slowly adapting and adjusting to life without the daily reminder of your beloved's physical presence. Think about ways you can continue to nourish the love and relationship and keep the memory of your loved one very much alive in your life. Because your relationship and love will forever remain very much alive, continue to engage the energy and honor the relationship and bond into the future. It is okay to admit there is a hole in your heart, but that is not the end of your story. As opposed to thinking of your grieving process as something to complete, find meaningful ways to actualize and give expression to the goodness your beloved pet brought to your life and the qualities you most admire about them. Moving on in our lives is about continuing to honor your relationship in a way that recognizes and pays tribute to all the goodness they brought to your life. Become those very things you most admire about your companion animal and bring those qualities to life! By doing so, you create a living memory, allowing your companion animal to continue living on through you, through your thoughts, intentions, actions, etc. The notion of continuance reminds and validates to us that our love is on-going, that it is normal and healthy to stay connected to our loved ones, and keeps their presence very much alive in our life. It's not that you can't go on living without your beloved companion; it's that you will believe in them every day of your life.

Transcendent Function of Grief; We Are More Than the Pain of Our Suffering

As human beings, we are influenced by our experiences, both good and bad, and one cannot expect to go through a traumatic event and not be changed or shaped by it in some fashion. As anyone reading this book can attest to, the experience of losing a companion animal has the potential to assault human faith with indescribable savagery. Yet, in the wake of such assaults, some find the strength to rise above to become more than they anticipated themselves ever to be. Perhaps grief was the conduit to strengthen you in places where you needed strength and/or soften you in places where you needed to soften. As the result of going through a loss of such magnitude, you may have acquired inner strength and resolve that you never imaged you possessed; or perhaps you developed a greater capacity for compassion and empathy towards others. As you evolve through your personal healing from loss, think about how you have changed and how these changes can benefit both you and your own life and others' lives. Some examples of how we transcend our own suffering include:

- Where there was once silence, there may now be a voice, more confidence with more self- esteem.

- You have a greater appreciation for time and mortality.

- You don't sweat the small stuff and have a deeper understanding for what really matters in your life.

- You take time to pause and enjoy the simple pleasures of your life.

- You know it is okay not to be okay.

- You have more tolerance, compassion, and understanding for those around you.

- You have a greater capacity for empathy and can feel closer to others, especially those friends or family who have supported you in your time of need.

- New friendships may develop because of your loss, perhaps a supportive coworker or neighbor, or new connections made in a support group.

Loss can break us so that we have no choice but to rebuild ourselves from the bottom up and "fix" some things along the way. The loss of our companion animal can show us a strength and resilience we may not have known we have. It can create opportunities for us to surprise ourselves with the things we can do and the things we can endure. Whatever your transcendence looks like, your newly founded qualities and attributes have the potential to bring about a slightly different version of yourself and change the way you engage with your life and the world around you. Grief is not something you accomplish or need to push through to go back to your old self. Grief changes your perspective; you see things differently, and you discover a new version of yourself. It is in the face of life's misfortunes and seemingly darkest moments, such as that seen in grief, that there exists the opportunity for personal and spiritual transformation. A quote by my former professor and Buddhist Psychologist Ronald Alexander, Ph.D. (2005) sums it up nicely:

> All of life's conflicts can be described as a struggle between letting go or holding on, opening to the present, or clinging to the past. Life's journey is a series of challenges that confront the self with difficult yet highly purposeful choices.

> The Ego clings to the "familiar" long after the nourishment has run dry. At that point, we face our deepest fears and truths. Our matriculation through the mystery of life asks that our soul awaken, take courage, and choose a more passionate and creative life.

Sometimes wholeness resides in the cracks and cervices where we thought hope was lost or pain was too great. Our experience of surviving the loss of our companion animal has the potential to open our eyes to reimagine what it means to be made new; to transcend our pain and suffering and become whole again not **because** of our loss but in **spite** of our loss. The difference in how we grow and rebuild from this tragedy maybe not in our breaking but in our mending. When we are called to enter a journey with no road map or means to light our shadowed path, we inevitably develop the capacity to endure and withstand the darkness and the strong winds that blow. As a result of our being in the journey as opposed to sidestepping the journey, we make our way through and come out on the other side never quite the same but changed as a result; possibly changed in ways that may bring us closer to the divine nature we find in our beloved companion animals. As noted by Animal Activist Stacy Andris, "we become their 'paws' in this realm," so allow their spirit to shine on through YOU, forever bound by that golden thread of love that connects you to your beloved. In your state of continuance and moving on together, become a reflection of the sacredness they brought to your life. May this be our ever-lasting tribute to all of the deeply treasured companion animals that have graced our lives. May you forever walk in the richness of the treasured gifts bestowed to you by them. Peace to you.

Below are journal questions and prompts to help you process your thoughts and feelings around Transcendence and Continuance:

To help cultivate continuance in your grief journey, create a list of all the attributes and characteristics you most admire about your beloved companion animal. Reflect on how you can continue to bring those virtues forth into the world through your actions and intentions.

Some ways that I can take the pain of my suffering and help those in need in honor of you are:

_____

_____

_____

_____

_____

_____

Knowing it is okay to continue in my life, some ways that carry you with me as I evolve in my life:

_____

_____

_____

_____

_____

_____

_____

_____

Knowing my love for you is greater than my grief, these are some ways that I can continue to honor you and all you brought to my life:

_____

_____

_____

_____

_____

_____

_____

Some of the ways I have changed for the BETTER since you died are:

_____

_____

_____

_____

_____

_____

_____

Some of the ways that I can continue to sustain a relationship with you as I move forward in my life:

My Reflections on Transcendence and Continuance

Real Life Vignettes of Transcendence and Continuance

Following are real-life narratives taken from clinical, research, and book interviews that highlight Continuance and Transcendence discussed in this chapter. These are just a few examples of how grieving pet owners describe their experience and perhaps you might find validation, hope, and connection through these brief stories.

Carol L and Canine Companion Chelsea:

I think because of this experience, I have become a different person. I see things about myself that have certainly changed and for the better. For one, I speak up and have a voice. I did not do that when Chelsea was alive and dying. I was so passive. Now I am much more assertive and I speak my mind in all parts of my life. Maybe I am trying to make up for not having that voice when she was dying, but now I do have a voice and stand up for myself for the first time in my life. I think I am stronger and wiser because of what I went through. If I can survive her death, I can survive anything. It has also taught me never to take anything for granted, and I wake every morning with a new and different perspective on life. I appreciate life much more, and I think I now see the world as Chelsea use to see it. So maybe my new way of being is not just from what I went through but also what Chelsea gave me; a sort of gift in her passing.

Julianne C. and Canine Companion Cecilia:

It's hard for me to think that any good could come out of something so bad, but after almost two years I believe it has. Because of how Sunny died, I took a stance for changes in terms of how

Veterinarians view the bond we have with our companion animals. I fought for Sunny even after she passed, which resulted in some very significant changes at the hospital. I wrote letters, filed complaints, and had meetings; I did everything I could to make sure other pet owners would never have to go through what I went through. So, looking back, I think I found a higher purpose to all of the pain and found an outlet to make some good out of it. That was my gift to Sunny. It is hard to find that silver lining, but being the conduit to elicit much-needed change in how companion animals are treated in end-of-life issues. I am not the same person I was before this happened. This experience has forced me to step out of my comfort zone and look at life, love, and loss so differently. I now look at each day with such respect, and I have become much more compassionate to others who are suffering. I guess you could say I have gone through a personal and spiritual transformation that benefits me and those around me. It is like I walked through fire and came out on the other side, changed in ways that perhaps I needed to change.

Marie L. and Canine Companion Penny:

One of the reasons I wanted to be a part of your book is that I wanted some good to come out of my experience of losing Penny. I wanted others to hear and understand what it is like for grieving pet owners. If through her death and my experience others can learn, then something good has come out of it. I will continue to find things to do in her memory that will help others because that was her nature to help others. In that sense, I have changed by being more giving, more patience, and understanding than I ever have. Those are the things that Penny was that I was not. This experience has really humbled me. I never felt such vulnerability, but now that has turned into something positive, and for that, I can thank Penny. In both her life and in her death, she taught me well. By being those things that she was in her life, I am keeping her alive in me, in a sense transcending the pain and suffering of her death.

Nick C. and Canine Companion Maddy:

Through this experience, I have changed in a way that I did not think was possible. This experience was like a catalyst for much-needed change. In one word. Control. I no longer hang onto control for dear life. Control was stripped from me when Maddy got sick and died. Because of that, I have been more open and engaged in life. I am able to take in the good along with the bad. It was as if I had been stripped of everything I had known and had to start from scratch. I have been humbled by this loss, greatly humbled. I never thought anything positive could ever come out of such a dreadful experience, but for me, looking back on who I was before and who I am now, I really like who I am now. Yet another gift from Maddy. I take her with me as I walk through my life; she continues with me as a gift of eternal love.

Marcie S. and Canine Companion Shayna:

I feel like the experience of losing Shayna has changed me. I've always been an emotional person who feels things deeply, but I think that part of me intensified after her death. I can't watch a movie or a video about dogs without becoming very emotional. It just kicks up those feelings, I suppose. My Dad recently had a goldfish die, and I burst into tears when we noticed him floating on the bottom of the bowl. Everyone, including myself, was curious and puzzled by my reaction. I suppose it was just the idea of losing a pet, no matter what type. It reminds me that life is finite, and it's important to stop and enjoy things whenever possible. We have another dog now that we love so much, and he's a little joy that brings us so much happiness. I try to make sure I stop and appreciate the little moments with him and never take them for granted. Like Shayna, I want him to have the best life possible; taking him places with us whenever possible, meeting and playing with other dogs, having a pampered life. I don't take anything for granted.

Natashia E. and Canine Companion Samantha:

I often felt as if it was a sort of punishment that my grief had been so long and so extremely difficult, but now, looking back, I can see how significant this experience has been for me. The person I have become because of this experience. I would never have become who I am today if not for this experience. I found and uncovered parts of myself that I never even knew were there. It feels like I am touching something within yet beyond myself, and it is so transforming. The strength I needed and developed through my grieving process was profound. My sense of empathy and compassion became a guiding force in my life. It has softened me where I needed to be softer and strengthened me where I was weak. My Samantha continues to transform me and my evolving self even through her death. Also, I created a charity in her honor that donates money to animals in need; through these efforts, she continues to touch others' lives as she did in her life as a Therapy Dog.

Memorializing Your Companion Animal and Creating a Ritual of Remembrance

Ceremony and ritual are the most common universal practices to memorialize the life and death of a deceased loved one. Memorial services bring healing to us and help facilitate the grieving process because they call to mind the full reality that our loved one has died and helps to process feelings of shock and disbelief immediately following the loss. When a human loved one departs this life, there are cultural, religious, and/or spiritual formalities to help gently and lovingly guide us by commemorating them. However, when our companion animals die, there are no recognized guiding principles to aid us in publicly memorializing and mourning our loss in the same way we do after the death of a human loved one. As grieving pet owners, we are left to our own devices to find ways to pay tribute to our cherished companion animal. We are marginalized from community supports typically available after the death of a human loved one and not given the opportunity to engage in funerals, life celebrations, memorial services, visitations, etc. Given that the healing aspect of memorializing our companion animals is not available to us, there can be serious implications on our emotional and psychological well-being, difficulty accepting the finality of the death, and can lead to increased isolation and loneliness typically not experienced during human loss or at least not to the same degree. This is an important factor in understanding why a companion animal's death is an extremely difficult and traumatic loss for many people and why it is essential to create a remembrance ritual.

Taking part in both public and private ceremonial activities is an essential and healthy part of your grieving and healing process. By its very nature, memorial services draw the death into the present and gives you the time and emotional space you need to reflect on the many ways your companion animal has graced your life, allows you to express affection and gratitude towards your companion animal offers you emotional comfort, sympathy, and support from others, and is an opportunity to share your sorrow and talk about our loss. By memorializing your companion animal, you are granting yourself sacred time for reflection and emotional recovery. Give yourself permission to commemorate and memorialize your beloved companion animal with some of the ideas below:

- Hold a memorial service at a place special to your companion animal where a poem, prayer, or eulogy can be read.

- Plant a tree, bush, and/or create a memory garden of your companion animal with a memorial stone.

- Donate money to a cause or charity that has significance to your beloved.

- If cremated, sprinkle the ashes in a special place and/or place in a personalized urn.

- Consider a butterfly release ceremony in their memory.

- Place a candle in the food bowl and light it during feeding times.

- Have a piece of jewelry made from your beloved's ashes or photo.

- Place an indoor plant, such as a Bodhi tree, in the water bowl to symbolize your continued love.

- Create a memorial photo album or scrapbook as a special keepsake of memories.

- Create a "memory" box with special and meaningful items belonging to your beloved companion animal.

- Have a balloon release ceremony and write messages on the balloons before releasing them to the sky

- Especially for children, write a letter and "send to heaven" if you have spiritual beliefs.

- Volunteer at a Shelter to honor your loved one's memory. By helping animals in need, your beloved continues to positively impact the lives of those less fortunate.

- Create a key chain from your companion's tag, as this was probably one of the first items you purchased for your beloved companion animal.

- Tattoos can be a lifelong linking object that connects you to your beloved and reminds you of your special bond shared.

Although these memorial ideas may seem simple, don't under estimate their significance. Their function is to create an avenue by which the memory you have and love you continue to feel is offered expression in a healthy and sustaining way in the present moment. Memorializing your companion animal is an expression that links you to him or her and is a symbolic integration of the essence of your relationship. Those who are grieving cannot raise the dead or change the laws of nature. However, by performing your own public or private ritual, you can regain your footing in a world that has become emptier than it was before. May you find peace and comfort in your tributes.

Ideas for Writing A Eulogy for Your Companion Animal

1. Write a brief chronological summary of the significant events that occurred throughout your companion animal's life.

2. Make a list of some of the things important to your companion animal, such as; favorite activities, favorite toys, favorite places, funny stories, etc.

3. Write a list of special memories, stories, and qualities of your companion animal

4. Combine all your thoughts, ideas, comments, and memories into one giant list.

5. Bring it all together with a personal touch that is reflective of your relationship.

My Eulogy to You:

My Eulogy to You:

CHAPTER FOUR:

Summary of Tips for Coping with the Loss of a Companion Animal and Other Helpful Thoughts

F ollowing is a summary of some of the tips and suggestions for coping with the loss of your companion animal found throughout this book, as well as some helpful thoughts and topics that might be of interest to you.

- **Acknowledge Your Loss:** Many times, grieving pet owners identify with the messages received from well-meaning friends and family that it was "only" or "just" a dog/cat, etc. It does not matter what the loss is; what matters is the nature of your bond and relationship, individual psychological constitution, and personal history that shapes your grieving process. No person has the right to minimize your loss, and the best thing you can do is permit yourself to acknowledge that the grief is real and you have the right to mourn the loss.

- **Address Feelings of Guilt:** It is quite possible as a pet owner you needed to make the extremely difficult decision of euthanasia. It is natural to struggle with feelings of guilt at having to make that choice for your beloved pet. When feelings of guilt emerge, try to reframe your thoughts around euthanasia as a final gift of love to spare your beloved pet from suffering the very difficult end stages of the dying process. Reminding yourself that you have lovingly and humanly allowed for a peaceful end to your beloved pet's suffering may help you cope with feelings of guilt.

- **Reach out to Others and be Honest:** Find "safe" friends that understand your pain and whom you are comfortable talking to about the loss. Don't pretend things are okay when things are anything but! Be honest with yourself and others regarding your true feelings. Holding in your true feelings leads to maladaptive ways of coping!

- **Consider Joining an online or in-person Pet Loss Support Group:** An in-person or online support group is a great way to openly share and discuss your feelings with others who have lost a beloved companion animal and understand what you are going through.

- **Be patient with Yourself:** While there are stages commonly experienced after a pet's death, grieving is very much an individual process. There is no timeline to "get over" the loss, nor does grieving occur in a linear fashion – you may find yourself going back and forth from one stage to another for quite some time. It is important to respect your own pace and not feel rushed to work through your sorrow and reconcile your loss. Give yourself permission to deal with your grief for as long as you need to, and don't feel compelled to throw things away (in attempts to throw the pain away) or get rid of reminders. If there are muddy footprints on the back window or in the car and fur on the floor or their bed and you're not ready to give them up yet, then don't!

- **Journal Therapy:** Some people find journaling to be a safe and effective way to process and gain insight into their feelings, especially when it is too difficult to open up and speak about the loss to others.

- **Recount the Details:** Early on after the loss, you may find that you need to repeat the details of the death over and over. This is okay and very natural as doing so helps to con-cretize the trauma and brings a sense of reality to the loss. Recite and recount what has been lost as often as you need.

- **Come to Terms:** Eventually, you will be able to face the re-ality of "death" squarely in the face by calling it what it is. Challenge yourself to name it, spell it, etc. This helps bring the reality of the death to the here and now.

- **Stop Avoiding and Begin to Gently Confront Reminders:** Gently confront reminders as opposed to avoiding them. This includes things like people and situations that you as-sociate with your deceased pet, looking at old photos and videos, visiting the grave, or viewing the ashes. Visit special places you have gone to together, touch toys, blankets, and other belongings.

- **Linking Objects:** Create and surround yourself with "link-ing objects" during the early stages of your loss. These are your deceased pet's items that help to remind you and cre-ate a sense of closeness to them. Having these "linking ob-jects" close by can help provide a sense of comfort that can be helpful early on after the loss.

- **Take Steps to Re-engage in Life Again:** At some point in your grieving process, you will begin re-engaging in life in a way that includes finding new ways to socialize, get involved with community service, keep a journal of the good things that have happened since the death.

- **Memorialize and Commemorate:** If not done so already, have a memorial service for your beloved pet. It is important to find ways to commemorate your pet, as this is an active way to grieve our loss and remember our loved ones. Please see chapter three for ideas for memorializing.

- **Give Yourself Permission to Mourn the Past While Living in the Present and Construct a New Sense of Self.** It's heartbreaking to realize the days of sharing your life with your companion animal are gone, most certainly a deep and unspeakable sadness. It is common to alternate between the "you" grieving your past and feeling like you are losing parts of yourself and your old life little by little, and the "you" engaging in your current life, growing, changing, and evolving. While straddling these two opposing worlds, it is possible to merge your past AND your present to construct a new sense of self and purpose. Although these two 'selves' may seem to be in direct contradiction to each other, realize that you have the ability to be both at the same time and that you are a work in progress, always evolving. Remind yourself that it is possible and healthy to mourn your past while still being grateful for and engaged in the present.

- **Accept that guilt can be a consequence of re-engaging in life again and can pressure you to stay in the past.** Guilt is one of the most powerful and crippling of all human emotions; it is the greatest destroyer of our emotional energy. Whenever you feel 'guilty' about doing things in the present without your companion animal, replace your guilt with a memory of happy times and cherished moments of your beloved. Carry the love you have for your beloved companion animal WITH you as you continue on in your life.

- **Remind yourself that even though your relationship has changed, it is still a relationship;** It is okay and healthy to have an ongoing connection with your companion animal. Yes, the relationship has changed, but it is nevertheless still a relationship; remember, death ends a life, not a relationship. Allow the emotional presence embodied within you to continue to inform your life in positive ways. Doing this can help lessen the pain of grief and maintain your connection. Love is stronger than death and stronger than grief; allow the love you continue to have to inform your life as you work towards re-engaging and adjusting to life without your companion animal.

- **Make a list of all the qualities you most admire about your companion animal.** From that list, envision ways that YOU can continue to bring those attributes and qualities forth into the world. In doing so, you create a "living memory" of your companion animal, and they will continue to live on through your actions and intentions. Remember, "moving on" is not about "leaving behind" or "letting go"; it's about continuing to honor your relationship in a way that recognizes all your beloved brought to your life and the world. What better way to do that than become the things you most admire about them!

- **Chose a few momentous "linking objects" to carry with you.** Linking Objects are items that "link" us to our deceased loved one. They are items that belonged to our deceased companion animal and remind us of positive experiences and feelings and help to comfort and give us peace. They are powerful and symbolic items that help you stay connected to them as you begin re-engaging and adjusting to life without their physical presence by your side.

- **Find a meaningful way to commemorate the death of your beloved and memorialize his or her life.** While culturally embedded, memorializing is something most of us do after the loss of a human loved one without thought or question. It is vital to our grieving process because it allows us to pay tribute to and honor our cherished companion animals. Memorials and ceremonies also serve to draw the death into the present moment and encourage you to be more present to the here and now, which can help if you are having difficulty re-engaging in life or feeling stuck in the past. See Chapter Three for ideas and suggestions on memorializing your companion animal.

- **Find "safe" friends that understand your pain and that you are comfortable talking to about the loss.** Since you may not be feeling or are feeling numb at this very early stage, you may not talk about your *feelings,* but talking about the *death and circumstances* surrounding your loss can be helpful.

- **You may need to repeat the details of the death over and over.** This is healthy and natural as it helps to concretize the trauma and bring a sense of reality to the loss. Recite and recount what has been lost as often as you need.

- **Don't pretend things are okay when things certainly are not!** Be honest with yourself and others regarding what you are feeling or not feeling. It is better to talk about it than keep it in; pretending everything is okay does not make everything okay and, in the end, will only make your grief much more difficult to work through.

- Eventually, you will be ready to face the reality of "death" squarely in the face by calling it what it is. Challenge yourself to say it, name it, spell it, etc.

- Gently and slowly confront reminders as opposed to avoiding them. This includes things like people and situations that you associate with your deceased companion animal, look at old photos and videos, visit the grave, view the ashes, visit special places you have gone to together, touch toys, blankets, and other belongings.

- Create and surround yourself with "linking objects" during this stage. These are items of your deceased companion animal that helps to remind you of your special bond and aids you in feeling connected and close to them. Having these linking objects close by can help provide a sense of comfort that can lend itself to gently merging out of the shock and denial stage.

Tips for Coping with Grief During the Holiday Season

The holiday season is meant to be a time filled with collective joy, happiness and goodwill, yet it may feel like anything but for the grieving! For those struggling with the loss of a beloved companion animal, the holidays' arrival can feel more like a pretty gift box filled with grief triggers than a time of celebration. The holiday season is a sad reminder that our furry bundle of joy is no longer here, and the traditions that once served to nourish us may set us into a spiral of painful feelings. It is natural and expected for the holiday season to trigger a wide range of emotions for those who have lost a loved one. Even in the absence of grief, our friends and relatives often think they know how our holidays should look, what "the family" should and shouldn't do. This dynamic can become even more amplified for those grieving the loss of a loved one. Below are some tips to help you navigate through the upcoming holiday season. Not all may resonate with you but pick ones that feel authentic to your healing process.

- **Set realistic expectations for yourself.** If this is the first year without your cherished companion animal, remind yourself that this year is and will be different. Do a personal inventory to determine if you can still handle the holiday's normal responsibilities and tasks that you've assumed in the past. Take a candid look at the events of celebrating and ask yourself if you want or can continue with the same traditions this year. If it feels over-whelming, then enlist the help of a friend or family member to help navigate through the holidays or permit yourself to change things up this year in a way that feels more manageable to you.

- **Set healthy boundaries and take a measured approach to Holiday commitments.** It is in the service of self-care to avoid circumstances and celebratory events that you don't feel ready to handle. You certainly should not force yourself to engage in every holiday event or celebratory tradition. If attending or engaging in certain events is likely to bring about too many painful memories, then be willing to say no. Other people may try to convince you to participate, but you certainly don't have to please everyone, and you are entitled to put your needs first. Pick and choose, very carefully, which events you are comfortable attending but try not to isolate yourself too much as that can intensify feelings of depression and sadness. While it is critical to carve out some time for reflection, remembering, and grieving, balance it with some activities with others.

- **Ask for help**. Many times, people are hesitant to ask others for help. You should not hesitate to ask for help when you're struggling and feeling emotionally overwhelmed with the holidays. Reminding loved ones that you're having a difficult time may be enough. Still, you may also need to reach out for additional support. Some people are uncomfortable with loss or do not know how to support grieving people, especially with disenfranchised losses such as the death of a pet. Look for in-person or online grief support groups or contact a professional counselor to help you cope more effectively with your grief during the holiday season.

- **Take special care of yourself.** Avoid using alcohol or other unhealthy means to self-medicate your mood as this short-term "solution" will only serve to make matters worse in the end. Instead, engage in self-soothing activities such as; physical exercise to help combat depression, writing in a journal to provide a good outlet for your grief, practice mindfulness, yoga, and stress reduction techniques to help reduce your stress reaction. Consider treating yourself to something that feels nurturing to yourself, such as a mini getaway, spa day, massage, etc.

- **Create a new tradition or ritual that is reflective of your current situation.** Some people find comfort in old traditions as it helps them feel closer to their loved ones, while others find those traditions too painful to carry out. Don't hesitate to create new traditions this year. Give yourself permission to be creative and do something out of the ordinary. You can also modify old traditions and make them fit better with this new era of your life. For example, you may ask family members to donate to a charity or cause relevant to your loved one in place of gifts; you can volunteer at a shelter or choose a specific day during the holidays in celebration and dedication to your loved one.

- **Focus on what you can control and let go of what you cannot.** There are many things about the holiday season that you cannot control, such as; Christmas music, decorations, holiday parties, etc. While you can't prevent those things from happening, think about and focus on some things you can control to make things more manageable. It's perfectly acceptable to limit your decorations or shop for presents online if going into the store triggers intense grief and sadness. Identify a few things you can do to assert some control over the holiday atmosphere and design a holiday plan that is best suited for your emotional needs.

- **Plan ahead, set limits, and have plan A /plan B options.** Often, the anticipation over how difficult something will be is much worse than the actual event itself. Are you reacting to the anticipation or the event? While a Holiday gathering may only last a few hours, you could easily spend weeks leading up to the event worrying about it. It can be helpful to establish a "breakaway" plan. For example, drive yourself to holiday functions or ride with a friend who will take you home whenever you feel that you have had enough. Just knowing you can choose to leave at any time may help ease your worries and allow you to enjoy the activity much more than you would if you felt stuck. Plan A is you go to the holiday gathering or dinner with family and friends. If you do not feel right, have your plan B ready. Plan B may be looking through a photo album, going to a movie, going to a special place you would spend time together or just go home and spend time with a friend. Many people find that when they have an option of Plan B, that is enough of a safety net to help them cope.

- **If all else fails, cancel the holiday altogether and find a different way to engage with the season.** Yes, you can indeed choose to cancel the holiday. If you push yourself to go through the motions but feel too overwhelmed by constant sadness or other painful emotions, you can cancel the holidays. Give yourself permission to take a year off from the holidays and tend to your needs in a self-nurturing way. Think of creative ways to "be" and engage during the holiday season that may not include gatherings and celebrations. Assess what elements of the holiday season you take pleasure in and what parts you don't. Just as there is no right or wrong way to grieve, there is no right or wrong way to handle the holidays while grieving, and only you can decide what is right for you. Permit yourself to change your mind about how and if you will celebrate the holidays in a way that is not informed by guilt or expectations of those around you. Do what is right for you and be honest with others about your own needs!

- **Find ways to honor the memories of your loved one and externalize the loss**. Create a special way to memorialize your companion animal during the holiday season. Finding ways to honor your loved one can serve as a tangible reminder that although your loved one is no longer physically with you, your love for them continues. Some ideas to consider are;

- Create a memory box and fill it with special photos of your loved one, letters, a eulogy, or precious keepsakes and mementos.

- Make a decorative/holiday quilt or have one made using items that remind your loved one.

- Place a bouquet of flowers or plant on your holiday table in memory of your companion animal.

- Place a commemorative ornament on the Christmas/ Chanukah/Holiday tree.

- If putting up a Holiday tree is too painful, consider calling it a "Memory" tree.

- Dedicate one of the Chanukah candles in memory of your loved one.

- Write a poem or share a favorite or funny story about your loved one and read it during a holiday ritual.

- Have a moment of silence or prayer before the holiday dinner in memory of your companion animal.

- Light a candle each night in honor of your companion animal.

- Create an online tribute for them.

- Volunteer at a place that holds personal significance and is symbolic of your relationship with your companion animal.

In summary, during the holiday season, be gentle with yourself, don't do more than you want or can and don't do anything that does not serve your healing process and feelings. Be sure to allow time to feel and express your feelings; don't keep emotions bottled up. If you have 1,000 tears to cry, don't stop at 500. Be open to allowing others to help, as we all need help at certain times in our lives. Remember, there is no right or wrong way to celebrate the holiday season after a beloved companion animal's death. The best way to cope with that first holiday season is to plan ahead, get support from others, and take it easy.

Changes of Season and Grief

It is very common for those struggling with grief to experience an increase in the severity of symptoms during the arrival of Autumn. I believe we are in tune with the natural rhythm of the seasons, and Autumn is a mirror to the seasonal changes within our own lives. Autumn is about endings; a very natural and organic process. The leaves that were once green and vibrant turn to brown and shed from the tree, reminding us to look at what we can or need to release and let go, which of course, can intensify symptoms of grief and loss. Every journey, every life, must come to an end, and Autumn is the bittersweet embodiment of this realization. Autumn teaches us about the importance of embracing change, letting go, and acknowledging all of life's impermanent nature. Autumn brings home the reality of death and challenges us to live each day to the fullest and walk through our day with a sense of mindfulness and gratitude. Autumn also calls to us to be reflective and prepare ourselves for the long winter ahead, when we all undergo an internal transformation. During the Autumn season, when we are reminded of the cycle of life and death inherent in nature and feel it within ourselves, we know that it is natural for this to trigger our grief reaction to things and loved ones gone from our lives but forever in our heart.

About Dr. Julianne Corbin

D
r. Corbin is a renowned and recognized expert on the psychological underpinnings of the human-animal bond and companion animal loss. Dr. Corbin earned her Ph.D. in Clinical Psychology from Pacifica Graduate Institute and is a New Jersey State Licensed Professional Counselor, National Board-Certified Clinical Counselor, Educator, and Researcher with over 20 years of diverse clinical experience in counseling and psychotherapy. Her area of clinical specialization focuses on; the human-animal bond and companion animal loss, grief counseling, disenfranchised loss, complicated grief, traumatic loss, hospice counseling, and end-of-life issues. Dr. Corbin's lifelong love and passion for the human-animal bond, combined with the lack of professional support services available to grieving pet owners, led her to specialize in pet bereavement counseling. Dr. Corbin is the Founder and Clinical Director of Integrative Psychotherapy and Pet Loss Support Services of New Jersey, which offers a wide range of clinical, educational, and consultation services to bereaved pet owners, mental health professionals, veterinary hospitals, animal welfare centers, law enforcement, and military personnel on the psychological dynamics of the human-animal bond and pet loss.

Dr. Corbin's professional and personal interest in the human-animal bond and companion animal loss was the inspiration for her doctoral dissertation research: *A Phenomenological Study of Canine Loss and Grief Response: Clinical and Depth Psychological*

Implications (2006). This research investigated the relational dynamics between humans and their canine companions and what grieving pet owners experience when this bond is broken through death. Through her research, Dr. Corbin explored the applicability of current models of human grief for this process and created a psychological treatment model of grief specific to those suffering the loss of a canine companion that is now used as the go-to guideline for mental health professionals nationwide. In 2018, Dr. Corbin published, ***Beyond the Horizon: A Remembrance Journal for Healing the Loss of a Pet,*** which is a reflective and therapeutic journal for those grieving the loss of a companion animal and interested in journal therapy as a way to work towards healing and recovery

In addition to Dr. Corbin's work with the Human-Animal Bond and Companion Animal Loss, she provides psychodynamic psychotherapy, mindfulness-based interventions, and evidence-based treatment to adolescents and adults across the lifespan with specialized training and focus on; health psychology, chronic/ terminal illness, chronic pain syndrome, normative and traumatic life transitions, addictions, eating disorders and mood disorders.

Dr. Corbin's personal experience, passion, and love for animals is the continued inspiration for her on-going clinical, research, and publications efforts to raise awareness of the importance of the human-animal bond and the need for professional pet bereavement support services.

References

Beetz, Andrea, et al. "Psychosocial and psychophysiological effects of human-animal interactions: the possible role of oxytocin." Frontiers in Psychology 3 (2012): 234.

Corbin, Julianne C. "A Phenomenological Study of Canine Loss and Grief Response: Clinical and Depth Psychological Implications" (2006).

Harvard Health Publications. www.health.harvard.edu/DOG (2016)

Miller, Suzanne C., et al. "An examination of changes in oxytocin levels in men and women before and after interaction with a bonded dog." Anthrozoös 22.1 (2009): 31-42.

Odendaal, Johannes SJ, and Roy Alec Meintjes. "Neurophysiological correlates of affiliative behavior between humans and dogs." The Veterinary Journal 165.3 (2003): 296-30.

Made in the USA
Columbia, SC
04 January 2022

53400550R00150